The Classics and South African Identities

CLASSICAL DIASPORA

The Classics and South African Identities

Michael Lambert

BLOOMSBURY

LONDON · NEW DELHI · NEW YORK · SYDNEY

Bloomsbury Academic
An imprint of Bloomsbury Publishing Plc

50 Bedford Square	1385 Broadway
London	New York
WC1B 3DP	NY 10018
UK	USA

www.bloomsbury.com

First published in 2011 by Bristol Classical Press

British Library Cataloguing-in-Publication Data
A catalogue record for this book is available from the British Library.

ISBN: PB: 978-0-7156-3796-8
ePUB: 978-1-4725-1976-4
ePDF: 978-1-4725-1975-7

Library of Congress Cataloging-in-Publication Data
A catalog record for this book is available from the Library of Congress.

Contents

For my colleagues and friends in the
Classical Association of South Africa

Acknowledgements

I am especially grateful to my former colleagues, Peter Tennant and Cullen Mackenzie, for taking on my teaching load during the sabbatical leave granted by the University of KwaZulu-Natal (Pietermaritzburg) to complete this book; to Peter Tennant for his critical comments on the first chapter; to Catherine Woeber (English Studies, UKZN) for her comments on the third chapter, to colleagues in the Classical Association of South Africa for happily sharing their stories with me; to my indulgent parents for never questioning my desire to have a classical education.

Introduction

In his chairman's address to the Classical Association of South Africa at the University of Pretoria in 1997 ('The Classics in South African Society – Past, Present and Future'), Richard Whitaker suggested, in response to Derek Walcott's ambivalent attitude to his classical education, that this kind of self-questioning and critical response to the classical tradition would be appropriate in South Africa. Appropriate because of the notable failure of classicists in South African universities to attract black students to the Classics and, consequently, black classicists to the Classical Association.[1] Whitaker's warning is worth repeating: 'if we cannot do this, if Classics remains the preserve of a White enclave, then it is hard to see a future for the subject in South Africa' (1997: 13). More than a decade later, I offer this book as a self-questioning and critical response to the South African classical tradition.

Underpinning this book will be the following basic assumption: that academic disciplines in South Africa, such as the Classics, are deeply embedded in the power relations, which have existed and continue to exist between the different races which constitute South African society. Consequently, the history, and indeed the historiography, of the classical tradition in this country should be rooted in the political, intellectual and cultural milieux of the period of its reception and transmission. This has not been attempted before. In this respect, events in the history of the Classics in South Africa and discourses about a 'classical education' should be interpreted as part of the same continuum. As Leon de Kock discovered when he wrote *Civilizing Barbarians* (1996: 188), I too have found that, as I attempted to sketch in the political background to important moments in the history of the classics in South Africa (e.g. the foundation of the current Classical Association in 1956), it became increasingly difficult to disentangle the organization and the discipline from the turbulent politics of the period.

For the purposes of this book, I do not intend to write a chronological history of the reception of the Classics in South Africa. Rather I intend opening three windows on to its history, using the creation of identities as the theoretical lens through which to guide our peep into the past. First, the Dutch colonial and Afrikaner background to the formation of the Classical Association in 1956 and the role of the Classics in the cultural reinforcement of Afrikaner nationalist identities. Secondly, a close reading of a selection of inaugural lectures of professors of Classics at one example of an English-speaking 'liberal' South African university in the 1970s, to illustrate how British colonial identity was redeployed in public discourses about the role of the classics in *apartheid* South Africa, and in Victorian-style 'comparative studies'. Thirdly, reflections on the 'classics debate' among black intellectuals in the late nineteenth and early twentieth centuries, which reaches to the heart of African identities in response to the missionary enterprise at institutions like Lovedale (Wesleyan), Zonnebloem (Anglican) and Mariannhill (Roman Catholic).

Identities – the theoretical lens

I am not going to rehash here the considerable debates about identity and nationalism which feature regularly in cultural and political stud-ies, awash with the various post-isms which have come to haunt the academy: post-modernism, post-structuralism, post-colonialism. I am indebted to these theoretical positions in the following ways.[2]

I believe that identities, rather like gender and sexuality, are socially constructed in and by the various discourses into which we are social-ized. Each of these discourses, whether they are about race, nationalism, ethnicity, religion, gender or place, has a history and these histories are embedded in the ideologies which shape them (e.g. British colonial capitalism or African communalism or Afrikaner nationalism).[3] This does not necessarily imply that our subjectivities, our identities as individuals, are entirely determined by the discourses into which we are situated and that we are wholly pre-determined beings, whose identi-ties have been scripted in advance. As Woodward reminds us, 'identity also involves an understanding of agency and rational choice' (2002: ix). One can choose to identify oneself as a 'black South African', as Robert Grendon does (see Chapter 3), even if he was, genetically, of a mixed race background – a 'coloured', to use the racial categories devised by the *apartheid* state. In reaction to Boer atrocities perpetrated against black South Africans, Grendon, who served in the British forces during the South African War (1899-1902), also identified himself as a loyal British subject.[4] Grendon's *choice* of identities thus illustrates that it is possible to engage with identity discourses in a manner which endorses or interrogates them. In Chapter 3 I illustrate how Davidson Don Tengo Jabavu, a black intellectual who had internalized the voices of empire, uses his colonial education in the Classics to subvert the very discourses into which he had been socialised. Both Jabavu and Grendon reveal how it is possible to hold a number of identities simultaneously, how making sense of one's personal narrative may well involve ambiguities and ambivalences which are sometimes resolved and negotiated, and sometimes not, often at great personal cost.

The very use of words such as 'discourse' and 'narrative' reveals that language is at the very root of the creation of our identities. It is highly significant that the emergence of Afrikaner nationalism in the Cape Colony in the late nineteenth century should coincide with the struggle for the recognition of Afrikaans as a language independent from Dutch. Important too that this struggle would probably not have occurred without the aggressive Anglicization of the Cape by the British colonizers and the tyranny of the English language in legislative, educational and socio-economic discourses. In other words, the power relations prevailing in the Cape at the time, both at a parliamentary and local level, generated discourses about Afrikaner identities, mobilized in and around language. Both structuralist and poststructuralist theories of identity and subjectivity are grounded in the notion that meanings are generated within language and that language is *the* site where power is produced, contested and interrogated. Foucault's cratology, despite its weaknesses, is certainly borne out by South African political, social, economic and cultural histories: the much-cited *le pouvoir est partout* ('power is everywhere') and *le pouvoir vient d'en bas* ('power comes from below') encapsulate the relational and creative aspects of this cratology.[5] The capillary concept of power is very useful for understanding, for example, the background to the formation of the Classical Association of South Africa in 1956 and its links with the consolidation of Afrikaner nationalism during the Verwoerd era. As this process cannot be understood without *relating* it to British imperialism, colonialism and African nationalism, so identities, like constructions of gender and sexuality, are profoundly relational and unstable, rooted as they are in shifting power relations. The identities of Jabavu and Grendon (cited above) illustrate this superbly well. Two caveats are important: the first is that one must be wary of homogenizing constructions of identity – for instance, Cape Afrikaner identity in the late nineteenth century was very different from, let us say, Transvaal Afrikaner identity in the same period; the second is that Afrikaner, British and African identities are not discreet identities which are not deeply implicated in the other. In fact, it is precisely where the boundaries are marked and crossed (or not crossed) that these identities become particularly interesting. Furthermore, just as the identities I refer to are not closed off from one another, so it would be incorrect to suggest that there is a cleavage between the 'liberal' British colonial period and the 'fascist' Afrikaner nationalist regime: it will become abundantly clear that the foundations of the *apartheid* state were firmly laid in the 'liberal' colonial period.

Identities and the Classics

As a classicist, I believe that it is important to demonstrate, especially to a postmodern readership, how these debates about power, language, identity and subjectivity are not simply the stuff of postmodern theory, but are perceptively explored in ancient Greek drama. Consequently, in this introduction, rather than focus on the theories of the oft-cited Saussure and Derrida, Foucault, Spivak and Bhaba, I intend to foreground Aeschylus' wonderful play *Suppliants* to deepen this discussion about identity, the processes of identity construction (or identification) and language, and to make the theoretical lens through which we intend to gaze at the classical tradition in South Africa more precisely focused.

John Berger's remark that the quintessential experience of the twentieth century is migration (in Woodward 2002: 53) could not have more resonance in Africa now. Civil wars, tyrannical regimes, famine and disease in countries like Ethiopia and Eritrea, Somalia, the Sudan, the Congo, Liberia, Rwanda, Burundi, the Ivory Coast and Zimbabwe have generated a flood of refugees migrating across borders, desperately seeking security and food. In South Africa, since the new democracy of 1994, many immigrants from the rest of Africa have attempted to find this here: 'we have our Africanness in common, we supported your people in exile during the years of racist oppression, make us

10

feel at home' has become the immigrant's frequently-heard plea (Morris 1999:83).

However, for many of them, South Africa has been a hostile haven. Violent acts of xenophobia are common. Pejorative words have been devised in vernacular languages to characterize these black foreigners who speak strange tongues, wear strange clothes and 'take our jobs and women'. Many experience police brutality and all have to confront the bureaucratic behemoth that is Home Affairs.[6]

The experiences of black exiles and immigrants in South Africa raise crucial questions about identity. Migratory peoples carry with them a history, a narrative, to make sense of themselves. The signifiers of difference are imprinted on their bodies, on their clothes, on their tongues. They enter communities with histories and thus the long and often painful process of negotiating between histories begins, as they attempt to forge new identities which somehow embrace sameness, without jettisoning difference.[7]

The history of identities in South Africa is also a history of migrations and painful negotiations, constantly re-enacted. The migration of the Dutch and British colonialists to the Cape; the migration of the Voortrekkers from the Cape; the migration of black slaves from Dutch colonies in the East Indies to the Cape; the migration of Indian indentured labourers to the colony of Natal; the diaspora of African peoples (the *Mfecane*) within South Africa itself in the eighteenth and nineteenth centuries; the migration of European missionaries and explorers 'into the interior'; the migration of black South Africans from their homes into the ghettoes and reserves created for them; the migration of Dutch-speaking South Africans to the Netherlands for higher education; the migration of black intellectuals in the late nineteenth century to the United States and Europe for the same purpose; the migration of white English-speaking and Afrikaans-speaking South Africans to Oxford as Rhodes Scholars; the migration of the classical tradition from its home in Europe to the Cape.

Aeschylus' *Suppliants* engages brilliantly with migration, identity and the processes of identification.[8] In the first eighteen lines of the play, Aeschylus makes the Danaides, exiled women, tell us their story. They have fled their home at the mouth of the Nile in Egypt (2-4) and have sailed to Argos in Greece to avoid what they consider forced, incestuous marriages with their cousins, sons of their father's brother,

Aegyptus (8-10; 37-9). Their father, Danaos, had advised them to flee to Argos (11-15), from where, they say, 'our race began' through Io, their primal mother (50), the cow tormented by the sting of Hera's gadfly, but touched and quickened by the breath of Zeus (15-18). Other details in their exile narrative are revealed in the remainder of the opening chorus. They have come to Argos, armed not with weapons, but with the wool-bedecked branches of the suppliants (20-2), in which guise they appeal for the protection of the local gods and, in particular, of Zeus himself, the god of suppliants (25-7). The men from whom they have fled are violent and abusive (29-30; 80-2; 104-5). Like Tereus' wife, they grieve as exiles (74-6) for the home they are accustomed to (63-4). They are aware of their difference. Their cheeks have been warmed to soft-ness by the Nile (70); they speak a different language, referred to twice in the opening chorus (119, 130); they wear foreign clothes (121, 132); again they refer to their journey by sea (134-6).

In this opening chorus, Aeschylus discloses, with extraordinary psy-chological and emotional insight, often lost in the arcane jargon of poststructuralist theory, how these women refugees have already begun to construct their identities in exile, before they have actually met any Argives. The process of their identity construction foregrounds the reasons for their journey, as they justify their choice of destination, thus romanticizing remote origins, as Greek colonizers of Egypt return to a 'home' of the religious imagination. The Danaides' acute awareness of their difference is rooted in appearance and language. They recall their geographical home, the 'fine-sanded dunes of the Nile' (3-4) with nostal-gia. They choose sacred space outside Argos, which will offer them the necessary security to negotiate their re-entry into what they believe is their ancestral 'home'. In the construction of identity, notions of terri-tory, boundaries and frontiers are of supreme importance, even in an age before the invention of the nation state.

If this is how the Danaides construct themselves, how are they perceived by others and how does this affect their awareness of their identities? Before the entry of the Argive king, Pelasgus, Aeschylus introduces the crafty figure of Danaos, their father, who reinforces their awareness of themselves as helpless exiles. Be modest, be submissive, he advises, in your speech (194) and your looks (199), as befits foreigners (195) and foreign refugees (202). He constructs the Argives as vengeful and violent (201). He espies a heavily-armed Argive army rattling across the plains to meet them (180-3). Even though Danaos is uncertain of the army's intentions (186-7), he responds to what he perceives as xenophobic overreaction with an equally xenophobic generalization: this race is malignant and hateful (201).

When the Argive king enters, he immediately asks where the Danaides have come from as he establishes their difference by their clothes, thus echoing how the Danaides had perceived their own difference and thereby reinforcing it. Using the familiar Greek world as the unquestioned norm, he begins to situate their difference within the polarities with which he (and presumably Aeschylus) constructs the world: Greek and non-Greek, Helladic and barbarian. The exiles are clearly unGreek (234); their robes are barbarian (235); no woman from the Argolid or Hellas would be dressed like this (236-7). He then homes in on the political aspects of their difference: no *'proxenos'* ('representative of foreigners' 238-9), the ancient equivalent of 'no passport, no visa'.[9] The only 'sign' (234) to which he can relate is that of the suppliant branches. Again he uses the word 'Hellas' (243) to establish the distance between 'us and them' and thus reinforce the foreignness of the Danaides. After introducing himself and recounting in detail the extent of his rule (250-9), ironically to those who are without *lebensraum*, Pelasgus homes in on another, perhaps the essential, marker of difference: tell me about your *'genos'* ('race', in the sense of descent or lineage, 272).[10] When the women claim that their *'genos'* is Argive (274), the king finds this hard to believe and further contributes to the 'othering' of the Danaides by comparing them with Libyan women, women from Cyprus, nomadic Indian women in a land neighbouring Ethiopia and Amazons (279-89). In other words, the Danaides are women of colour. They have mentioned this themselves in the opening chorus (154-5). Pelasgus draws attention to their blackness, and from then on in the play, the colour of their skin becomes an important feature of their identities and that of their father, Danaos.

Later when Danaos asks Pelasgus for safe escort to the temples in the city, he reinforces the king's perception of his *'genos'* by saying 'the nature of my appearance is not the same' (496) – the Nile does not nurture a *'genos'* like that of Inachus. His daughters again use the word 'black' (530) of their violent cousin-suitors; Danaos then contrasts the black limbs of his brother's sons with their white garments (719-20); the Danaides refer to the onslaught of the black army pursuing them (745).

13

Blackness is thus associated with violence, abuse and rape.[11] Although the Danaides distinguish themselves from their black pursuers, as first cousins, whose cheeks have been warmed by the Nile, they are aware that they too are black.[12] However, as they stake their claim to Argive descent, they wish to distance themselves from the blackness of their Egyptian pursuers. They have adopted Pelasgus' perception of their difference. As he 'others' them by reinforcing the non-Argive nature of their appearance, so they 'other' their cousins by disdaining their blackness. Often exile identities are constructed by the racist xenophobia of host communities, which forces refugees to internalize negative perceptions of their difference. Self-denigration and alienation are created by others.

Race, clothes, language: another crucial marker of difference is the political system which shapes attitudes towards authority and responsibility. When the Danaides ask the Argive king to take their plea for asylum seriously (359-64), Pelasgus replies that he cannot promise anything until he has discussed the matter in council with all his citizens (368-9). But, retort the Danaides, 'you are the city, you are the people; you are sole ruler and decide everything' (374-5). As they come from Egypt, Aeschylus ensures that the Danaides are used only to authoritarian, tyrannical rule, in contrast to the obviously anachronistic democratic process which the Argive king appears to employ.[13] For these refugee women, returning 'home' will involve adjusting to a political system in which men consult rather than dictate.[14] Once again Pelasgus, fearful of the military consequences of supporting the Danaides, stresses the need for consultation with the people (398-9), as he dreads being accused of destroying the city because he harboured foreigners (401). Danaos, clearly a stranger to the democratic process too, reports to the Danaides that the Argive assembly voted unanimously by raising their right hands (607) to accept father and daughters into the city as free metics (609), but ambiguously and craftily represented to the assembly by Pelasgus as both guests and citizens (618).[15] In response to Danaos' news, the Danaides' prayer for Argos includes a strophe devoted to the Argive political constitution (698-703), in which they appear to have accepted that the people rule the city (699), yet clearly do not accept socio-political institutions like marriage.[16] The process of assimilation and adjustment to a new political system has begun. Aeschylus is fully aware how painful and difficult this process can be for refugees. When Pelasgus makes it clear, in front of the aggressive Egyptian herald, that the democratic constitution of Argos offers the Danaides a choice of public hospitality (957, cf. 1010-11) or private accommodation (961), the women ask their father's advice before choosing (966-72), specifically because 'people are prone to find fault with those speaking a foreign tongue' (972-4). Significantly, Danaos enters with a bodyguard which he requested (492-6),[17] granted by the Argives (985-6), and begins his advice with a variation on this perpetual fear of the refugee: everyone is quick to slander the '*metoikos*' or alien (994-5). Even though the Argives have voted to accept Danaos and his daughters into their community, there are clearly underlying fears, suggests Aeschylus, that this action may result in resentment and possible murder. In the context of this play, Danaos claims that he needs the bodyguard not to protect himself and his daughters from the Egyptians, but that he may have 'honoured privilege' (986) and may not be unexpectedly and secretly murdered (987-8). The host community appears to have accepted the refugees at enormous cost to itself (the threat of war), but Argos is not perceived as a utopian fugitives' haven. The leader of the refugees fears the threat of violence from within, which suggests that there is some ambiguity in the welcome and some unease attached to the status of metic in Argos. Perhaps a 'resident alien' with his eye on power and thus a need for henchmen generates fears. Not all immigrants are passive victims.

Territory, race, clothes, language, political system: there is a further element which makes the *Suppliants* so superb a reflection on the process of identity construction, and that is gender. As they make clear in the opening lines of the play, the Danaides are female refugees fleeing from what they perceive are the incestuous desires of their male cousins and led into exile by their father, who made the decision to flee to Argos (9-15). Throughout the play, Danaos controls their behaviour. He instructs them how to act as suppliants in as manipulative a manner as possible (188-202); he warns them, after they have been granted asylum by the Argives, not to shame him by being unchaste (996-1013). The Danaides themselves constantly conceive of their exile in gendered terms: women fleeing from the violent lust of men (28-30, 426-7, 528, 817-18) and the brutal enslavement of a forced and polluting marriage.[18] Aeschylus' intricate web of animal imagery further underlines the gendered nature of this exile and the ensuing pursuit.[19] Furthermore,

Pelasgus wonders whether the men of Argos should risk war 'for the sake of women' (477). When the Argives vote to accept the suppliants, the Danaides specifically refer to the vote in gendered terms: 'they did not vote with men, dishonouring the cause of women' (644-5). Pelasgus, ostensibly the supporter of the cause of these women, reacts to the arrogance of the Egyptian herald with a sexist taunt: do you think you have come to a city of *women*? (913). The herald explicitly conceives of the inevitable conflict as a battle of the sexes and prays for male victory and power (951).

In the final chorus of the play, the Danaides sing in praise of the city which has accepted them and reject their country of origin (1023-5). Conscious rejection of 'home' is perhaps important for the construction of a new exilic identity, but exiles do not easily abandon their emotional and psychological baggage: they carry it with them. In the choral song at the end of the play, the Danaides still express their fears of forced marriage with the sons of Aegyptus (1043-6; 1052-3; 1062-4). Amongst their final words is a request to Zeus to grant the women power (1068-9). Despite the safe haven provided by Argos, these women refugees know that they are still women, subject to the rule of their father, the power of the votes and stares of strange men in Argos and the power of the men from Egypt, still in hot pursuit.

There is no doubt that the experience of many African refugee women in contemporary South Africa resonates with that of Aeschylus' Danaides. The flight from sexual abuse, oppressive social and political systems and war, generated by men – the flight to what is perceived as a democratic haven and the consequent disillusionment when the host community turns out to require persuasion (like the Argives), or to offer an ambiguous welcome. This makes the attempt to forge new identities more painful, when one is prejudged or misjudged solely on the basis of one's appearance, language or different history. What makes the Danaides so interesting is the fact that they claim Argive roots, but do not look or sound Argive and their claims to Argive territory are thus unclear to the Argives. African refugees in South African have black-ness in common with the majority of South Africa's population, but do not look or sound South African. Hence the suspicion and xenophobia which confronts many of them when they move into the territory demarcated 'South Africa'.

The Greeks were arguably the first civilization to establish the category of 'other' or 'foreigner', using language as the critical marker of difference (hence '*barbaros*').[20] Many black South Africans frequently refer to immigrants from the rest of Africa as '*makwere kwere*', a derogatory term for black foreigner coined from the perceived sounds of their different languages (Morris 1999: 84, n.15). Aeschylus' Danaides are eventually compelled by their father to murder their husbands; initially the pawns in a brutal game of patriarchal manipulation, they become, with the exception of Hypermestra, murderers themselves. The victims of violence become its perpetrators.

A South African version

Support for this South African reading of Aeschylus' *Suppliants* has been provided by a dramatic version of the play which has already been staged in South Africa with the co-operation and support of African refugee women.

In 2002, the South African playwright Tamantha Hammerschlag, lecturer in Drama Studies at the University of KwaZulu-Natal (Pieter-maritzburg), explored exile, identity and xenophobia with a group of African refugee women at the Jesuit and Bienvenu Refugee Centres in Johannesburg. To do this, she produced her own version of the *Suppliants* which incorporated mythological material from what we know of the trilogy, introduced women who committed murder (Medea, Deianeira) or who were foreign immigrants (Medea) and juxtaposed the Greek mythological world with the grim prose of South African bureaucracy, in the form of official applications for permanent residence and official rejections. This version of the *Suppliants* was performed in Johannesburg at The Nunnery, University of the Witwatersrand, and was attended by the refugee women from the centres, whose narratives had contributed to the play.

One of Aeschylus' themes translated into a contemporary setting by Hammerschlag is that of language.[21] In the opening dialogue with Danaos, the nomadic Io reflects:

> I speak six languages. Every year I learn one more. Sometimes two or three. I speak the language of war. And still I fail to make myself understood. To learn how to buy bread. Which queue is for rations. How to bribe the officials. How to read the timetables. It takes so

much time. Walking this way and that – and then they cannot UN-DER-STAND you and they send you back again. So you have to start again. Stand in the queues. Get your photograph taken (Hammerschlag 1999: 7).

Once again, Io, in conversation with Danaos, returns to the theme of language and this time connects the acquisition of languages with the ideologies in which they are embedded:

Be careful. I speak six languages. I have travelled. Every country that opens it door to me has taught me something new ... every country teaches you ... something new about hatred. In each country it is different people for different reasons ... When I was a child I thought it was just us. My people, where I come from, were *so good* at hating. But as I travelled I learnt that was not true. If the gods could grant me one wish – ONE WISH. I would make them, make me unlearn that. Unlearn the language. Unlearn the hatred (ibid.: 25).

At the end of Hammerschlag's version, the Medea who has been raped and tortured says similarly:

I have travelled. I am applying to you here in Corinth for asylum. I speak many languages. With each crossing I learn another (ibid.: 52).

Language, as Aeschylus recognized, is at the heart of identity construction and the fractured identities of Hammerschlag's migrant women echo the narrative of the Danaides.[22]

As Hammerschlag appreciated, the subtle intricacies of the links between identity, power, race, language, religion and gender are conveyed more powerfully by Aeschylus' *Suppliants* than by any prolonged theoretical discussion. There is no doubt too that Aeschylus, in attempting to define dramatically what it meant to be a Greek, contributed to the invention of the 'barbarian' and, in attempting to define what it meant to be an Athenian, wove into his text propaganda for the relatively new democracy.

In the following analysis of the engagement of different South African communities with the classical tradition, I realize that in aiming the text at an international readership I may have blurred the subtleties and complexities of South African identity construction, by not achieving the appropriate balance between exposing the operations of power in educational discourses both at the 'macro' and 'micro' levels. I hope that in discussing identity and its construction of 'others', so fundamental to its existence, I may not have indulged in some Aeschylean 'othering' myself. I write as a white English-speaking South African male – that statement in itself implies a host of 'others', who may be offended by any attempt to circumscribe their identities. The only consolation I can offer is that confronting the ghosts which hover over our discipline in South Africa will, I hope, be a burden shared.

1

The Classics and Afrikaner Identities

In each people language, nationality and worship are very closely interconnected, so that if one is lost the others lose their power.
Dr Changuion, Dutch professor of Classics, South African College, 1857, quoted in Tamarkin 1996: 44

CASA's Golden Jubilee, 2007

In July 2007 the Classical Association of South Africa (CASA henceforth) celebrated its golden jubilee at its twenty seventh biennial conference, held at the University of Cape Town. The theme was 'Aspects of Empire' and, of the eighty-nine delegates, sixty-one were South Africans or foreign classicists working in South African universities; the rest were from the United Kingdom, France, Italy, the Netherlands, Greece, the USA, Canada and Australia. Of the South Africans, fewer than half were Afrikaans-speaking; there were no black South Africans present and no delegates from other countries in Africa.[1]

Before 1994 and the first democratic elections in South Africa, CASA's biennial conferences were markedly different in some respects. There were almost no foreign delegates, as many countries (certainly all of the above) actively supported academic and cultural boycotts of *apartheid* South Africa at least until the early nineties, and white Afrikaans-speaking delegates greatly outnumbered white English-speaking ones. In fact the executive committee of CASA is still dominated by Afrikaans-speaking South Africans (usually white males), as it has been since its inception in 1956.[2]

In one respect, however, the face of the CASA conference in 2007 and of those held before 1994 was depressingly similar: the virtual absence of black South African delegates, with the exception of an occasional South African classicist of mixed race, from the so-called

21

'coloured' community, who may or may not have identified himself/ herself as black.

The Foundation of CASA, 1956

The domination of CASA by Afrikaans-speaking white males is a legacy of the foundation of the organization at the University of Pretoria in 1956. Of the seventeen men present at the first meeting, the majority were graduates of Afrikaans-speaking universities or professional classicists working at them.[3] Many had completed doctorates at universities in the Netherlands;[4] a few were graduates of Oxford and Cambridge as well.[5]

Interestingly, perhaps significantly, the draft constitution of the organization had been sketched on board the *Durban Castle* by two of the founding members (van Rooy and Lubbe) returning to South Africa from studying in the Netherlands,[6] thus recalling an earlier Dutch expedition to the Cape of Good Hope in 1652, authorised by the Heren XVII (the directors) of the Dutch East India Company.

Dutch Classics at the Cape

The Dutch East India Company, or rather the VOC (Vereenigde Oostindische Compagnie), arguably the world's first multi-national corporation, eager to make profits for its investors, did not arrive to establish Classics or education of any kind at the Cape in the seventeenth century. Its 'modest' purpose was to establish a half-way house for the Company's ships en route to the East Indies, the source of the lucrative spice trade (Giliomee and Mbenga 2008: 42).

As the company's employees at the Cape were drawn from the middle and lower ranks of the burgher class (van Stekelenburg 2003: 90), Erasmus was not transplanted on to the Cape flats. What education there was seems to have been entirely expedient: making slaves profitable investments by teaching them the language and religion of the master. *Cuius regio, eius religio* indeed.

Jan van Riebeeck, the VOC official selected to supervise the establishment of the half-way house at the Cape, records in his diary (his *Daghregister*) that he established a school (1658) for the children of male and female slaves from Angola, confiscated from a Portuguese slaver by the Dutch ship, the *Amersfoort*:

... We have begun to make preparations for the establishment of a school for the Company's Angolan slave children from the *Amersfoort* ... which school will be held in the morning and afternoon by the sick comforter and sick visitors teaching them the correct Dutch language. To animate their lessons and to make them really hear the Christian prayers each slave should be given a small glass [*croesjen* or *kroesje*, a mug or cup] of brandy and two inches of tobacco etc. A register must be established and names should be given to those who do not have any names. All slaves, couples or singletons, young or old, will be under the personal aegis of the Commander. Within a few days, these slaves will be brought under a proper sense of discipline and become decent people.[7]

It is indeed an irony, considering the subsequent history of education in South Africa, that the first school founded by Western settlers should have been for the children of black slaves. Clearly neither Latin nor Greek was taught at this school, but, predictably, Dutch, and a Calvinist version of Christianity endorsed by the Synod of Dordrecht (1618-1619), which shaped the religious and pedagogic principles of all teachers in and from the Netherlands (Behr 1952: 67), especially after the protracted struggle with Catholic Spain for religious freedom. As Robert Shell remarks, van Riebeeck, with the foundation of this school, 'introduced education, paternalism, and the *dop* system (providing alcohol on a daily basis to servants and slaves) into the infant colony' (1994: 79).

Whether the Synod would have approved of the tot of brandy and the tobacco handed out to the pupils daily is doubtful. Abraham Behr, anxious to defend this practice of the Dutch East India Company, notes that in the East Indies 'rice was often given to pupils to attract them to school' (1952: 67). The lessons of the first schoolmaster, van der Stael (van Riebeeck's brother-in-law), the *sieckentrooster* (or 'sick-comforter'), clearly required analgesics of a less nutritious nature. Despite these incentives, the school was not a success. Five years later, his successor was teaching a grand total of seventeen pupils, of whom four were slaves, and the remainder whites and one Khoikhoi.[8]

Early education of the western variety at the Cape was thus rooted in the following principles which have shaped the trajectory of education in South Africa for centuries: imparting, or rather inculcating, the language (whether Dutch, Afrikaans or English), and the religion and values of the settlers and (later) colonizers. Van Riebeeck's desire to instil a 'proper sense of discipline' so that subject populations become 'decent people' effectively encapsulates the kind of education for subjection which characterized the educational systems during the British colonial period, and during the years of Afrikaner nationalist rule.

'A register must be established and names should be given to those who do not have any names.' Shell's statistical analysis of names given to slaves at the Cape in the period 1656-1762 indicates that 27.3% of the slaves in his sample were assigned names connected with the classical tradition, a higher percentage than Old Testament, indigenous, calendar and 'facetious' names (1994: 241). Shell notes 81 Tituses, 53 Cupidos, 50 Coridons, 35 Hannibals and 39 Scipios, apart from the many slaves named Mars or Venus (ibid.: 242). John Hilton's study (2004: 19-20) groups the slaves' classical names into categories (e.g. Literature, Philosophy, Mythology) and indicates that the majority of slaves' names were derived from Greek and Roman history and religion (Caesar, Pompeius, Augustus, Antony, Mercurius, Neptunus). Dutch slave owners' preference for names from the classical tradition probably reflects the influence of Roman models of slave-naming on the few educated owners who dictated 'fashion', and the dynamics of the market-place: by the time of van Reebeeck's arrival at the Cape, slavery was illegal in the Netherlands (1648) and the Company officials, ships' captains and slave traders thus resorted to Roman, rather than Dutch, naming practices (Hilton 2004: 27-34; Parker 2001: 7, 20).

However, in the minds of the slaves and the 'free' indigenous peoples, some of whom also received classical names, the classical tradition is thus inscribed, from the outset of its reception in South Africa, in relationships of dominance and subservience. It is notable that the classical names chosen by the slave owners have either martial (Mars, Titus, Hannibal, Scipio, Caesar, Pompeius) or erotic (Coridon/Corydon, Cupido, Venus) connotations, which suggests that the naming system, as an integral part of what Shell calls the 'hegemonic apparatus' (ibid.: 246), reflected the militarism which accompanied the process of colonization and the sexualization of the relationship of ownership: presumably pretty boy-slaves were originally named Corydon or Cupido and pretty girl-slaves, Venus. Hilton even finds a male slave with this name (2004: 23): one wonders whether this is a case of a poor classical education and/or sexual abuse on the Cape flats.

1. The Classics and Afrikaner Identities

Records of the Church council at the Cape indicate that in 1676 it was strongly felt that, in the light of the deterioration of moral and religious standards in the Slave Lodge – a windowless fortress 'run by Company officials on a military system' (Giliomee and Mbenga 2008: 53) – separate schools for white and slave children (black) should be established and suitable black teachers (fellow slaves, convicts or free blacks) found for the slave children (Behr 1952: 71-2). This was achieved in 1685 when the second slave school was established for the Company's black slaves only, its purpose being to teach Calvinist Christianity (prayers and catechism), reading and Dutch, especially fluent conversational Dutch, to slaves from continental Africa, Madagascar, India and Indonesia (Giliomee and Mbenga 2008: 53), in short, the territory which fell within the orbit of the Dutch East India Company.[9] 'Coloured' offspring of white fathers and black slave mothers had to go to the slave school as well, but the fathers had to pay fees (Behr 1952: 73-4): it was clearly not the slaves who were responsible for the deterioration of moral standards in the Lodge. Van Reede, a visiting commissioner in 1685, was appalled to find out that almost half of the children of Lodge slaves were 'descended from *Neder Duijtse vaders*' (Dutch fathers) (Shell 1994: 344). This is not surprising as the Lodge functioned, for an hour each night, as a brothel for the 'local garrison' (Giliomee and Mbenga 2008: 53).

In this context of the beginnings of segregated public education in South Africa, the first formal 'Latin School', rather like the elitist 'Latin Schools' of eighteenth-century Protestant Europe, was opened at De Kaap (later Cape Town) in 1714 (Smuts 1960:7), presumably for the white sons of Dutch, German and French Huguenot settlers only, although there is evidence that slaves attended public schools in the latter half of the eighteenth century.[10] By 1714, the refreshment station at the Cape had been transformed into a colony. The first Company servants had been released (the first 'free burghers') to establish farms, and a system of 'loan farms' had been instituted beyond the mountains, which resulted in the 'unsystematic colonization of the interior' and the consequent clashes with indigenous peoples (Giliomee and Mbenga 2008: 47, 62-3). Furthermore, a Muslim community had been established with the arrival of political exiles, convicts and slaves (ibid.: 69).

The 'Latin School' was thus founded in a multi-cultural context by the hegemonic, colonizing power, for the education of the sons of the colonizers. Significantly, the Rector of the school was a Reverend Lambertus Slicher of Middelburg, who had been an army chaplain, and was appointed by the Council of Policy of the Dutch East India Company. The language of education, was, of course, Dutch. This close link between the teaching of the Classics, the Netherlands and the church, especially the Dutch Reformed Church, is a constant theme in the history of classical education in South Africa.

But why a 'Latin School' at the Cape? Knowledge of Latin was still considered a mark of the educated and 'civilized' man, and the Dutch colonizers, perhaps more keenly aware of social mobility than their counterparts on the continent, wanted to equip their sons with the means to social advancement *back home*, and at the Cape, where Latin (like the classical slaves' names) had the effect of accentuating the gap between the 'civilizer' and the 'native' or 'slave' or Muslim, thus justifying the domination of the masters and the subjugation of the mastered. Furthermore, a knowledge of Latin was essential if one wanted to enter the legal profession, as legal practitioners at the Cape constantly referred to Roman law as interpreted by Dutch jurists, and in cases involving slaves, for instance, frequently cited as precedents actual Roman trials (such as Cicero's *Pro Milone* and *Pro Cluentio*) and Latin authors as varied as Tacitus, Valerius Maximus, Ovid, Juvenal and Aulus Gellius. As early as 1672, the Fiscal quotes directly from Justinian's *Digests* (with precise references), indicating the presence of a law library at the Cape 'which was considerably expanded in the eighteenth century' (Hilton 2007: 4).

This Latin school had closed by 1730, by which stage the population of European 'free burghers' had risen to 2,540 (Giliomee and Mbenga 2008: 59); a second was established, with the help of public donations, in 1793, entirely dedicated to the teaching of Latin and Greek through the medium of Dutch (Smuts 1960: 8). 1793 was also the year in which the first Muslim school or *madrasah* was established at the Cape (Giliomee and Mbenga 2008: 101).

In the years between the closure of the first and the opening of the second Latin schools, the area of European occupation in the Cape had increased tenfold, a class structure with a landed 'gentry' at the apex was firmly in place, a creolized language (Afrikaans) had taken root, the first European missionaries to indigenous blacks had arrived, and tensions had developed between the 'free burghers' and the mother country, and between the colonists and the Khoikhoi, San and Xhosa peoples (Giliomee and Mbenga 2008: 66-78, 98-9). In addition, the Dutch East India Company was in serious financial difficulties (it was dissolved in 1799), which probably accounts for the need for public donations to establish the school.

During the years 1730-1793, when the colonists, in contrast to the Muslim community, were not especially interested in formal education, sons of white settler families, in pursuit of a good school and university education, chiefly for the purposes of entering the church, felt that they had to go to the Netherlands. As the Reverend Vos laments in his memoirs:

> As there was at that time no Latin school in this country, not to speak of a University, I was forced, in order to become a minister of the gospel, to leave the land of my birth and go over to Europe (quoted in Smuts 1960: 7).

Another son of a settler family, Gysbert Hemmy, whose father was one of the many German employees of the Company, went to the Latin School in Hamburg, where he delivered, as his school-leaving *declamatio*, an *Oratio Latina de Promontorio Bonae Spei* (Latin oration on the Cape of Good Hope) in 1767 before proceeding to Leiden where his dissertation was entitled *De testimoniis Aethiopum, Chinensium aliorumque paganorum in India Orientali* (1770) (On the testimony of Africans, Chinese and other pagan peoples in the East Indies).

Hemmy's oration begins, in standard classical fashion, with three citations – from Vergil, Horace and Silius Italicus – to support his extravagant praise of the riches of India (perfumes, spices, ivory) and European trade with India, which had resulted in enormous benefits (for Europe, that is).[11] In his praise of the benefits brought by this trade with India, the twenty-one-year-old Hemmy comments on the founding of many colonial settlements which 'opened new avenues to power for many Europeans' (White 1959: 6), thus inadvertently providing us with one of the real motivations for Dutch colonization at the Cape: personal and national *potentia* (power). All this, of course, would have been impossible without the Portuguese and Dutch discovering the route round the Cape (ibid.: 7).

A tactful opening indeed for a scion of a loyal servant of the Dutch East India Company, who, presumably, would be seeking employment with the Company in the near future. Hemmy courts the Company with a fulsome *captatio benevolentiae*. Throughout his *oratio*, the Company is flattered with the epithet 'illustrious' (*illustris societas*)[12] and exonerated from any charge of exploitation: the Europeans have by 'fair purchase (*justissimo emptionis titulo*) acquired the Cape and adjacent territory' (ibid.: 11).

In his account of the geography of the Cape, its flora, fauna and its indigenous peoples, Hemmy is influenced by standard travel writings of the eighteenth century. The *oratio* clearly required him to display his scholarly research, and he does not disappoint his audience. He acknowledges his use of Peter Kolbe's *Caput Bonae Spei hodiernum* (The Cape of Good Hope today)[13] and *Die Allgemein Welthistorie* (The General History of the World), a compendium of eighteenth century travel writings,[14] which provide him with some extraordinary ethnography on the Hottentots (now the Khoikhoi), most of it a combination of stereotypes of the 'other' culled from classical authors such as Herodotus, Tacitus (his *Germania*, for instance), eighteenth-century myths about the 'noble savage' and, in the case of Kolbe's work, possibly from van Grevenbroek's positive account of the Hottentots.[15]

We are informed that the Hottentots, who are, of course, 'averse to hard labour', (*impatiens laborum*) have 'fingers ... equipped with little talons, like the claws of eagles' (White 1959: 7-8). Their women, surprisingly, possess 'pendulous breasts, which they can throw over their shoulders and offer to their babies' (ibid.: 8). Furthermore, although their religion conceives of a shadowy god of gods, dwelling beyond the moon, he is worshipped in the shape of the moon (ibid.: 9). Although they have no written laws, they seem to have a 'natural law', imprinted on their hearts (ibid.: 9). In fact, Hemmy is at pains to stress that 'in charitable deeds and hospitality to fellow-members of their race and to foreigners they are superior to many Christians' (*beneficentia et hospitalitate in cives suos et peregrinos multis Christianis antecellunt*, ibid.: 9). Insights are offered into tensions between tribes near the Cape who provide slaves for the company or private citizens or are farm workers, and forest and cave dwellers, who plunder civilized Hottentots. Cruellest of all are the Caffres, implacable enemies of the Hottentots (ibid.: 10).

In a footnote, Hemmy finds supporting evidence for Kolbe's extraordinary view that the Hottentots are descendants of the Jews and lists some specious similarities (ibid.: 11-12). The Hottentots also have their Adam and Eve (Nob and Hingnob), sacrifices of atonement, ease of divorce, primogeniture, and Levitican-style taboos regarding incest, menstruating and newly-delivered women, and the consumption of pork. Hemmy imagines that the Hottentot custom of excising the left testicle at puberty or when men are newly married suggests the Jewish rite of circumcision (ibid.: 12). In 'squalor and uncleanness' the Hottentots surpass the Jews. Clearly Hemmy's education in Hamburg, which had a Sephardic Jewish community from as early as the sixteenth century, extended to anti-semitism as well.

In the final section of the *oratio*, Hemmy returns to an encomium of the Cape's fertility, wonderful harbour and abundant wild life (ibid.: 14-16). He ends with a more detailed account of the Cape's discovery in which credit is given to the Portuguese explorers, Diaz and Vasco da Gama, although the Portuguese revenge on the Hottentots for the murder of their countrymen is given undue prominence (ibid.: 16-19). The reason for this prominence is soon revealed. Predictably, the speech ends, in contrast to Portuguese excesses, with an account of the orderly and civilized actions of the Dutch East India Company, in which van Riebeek buys land from the Hottentots 'at an agreed price' (*pretio constituto*) and the distinguished Directors of the Company establish law courts and build churches, thus displaying their great foresight (ibid.: 19-22).

At the suggestion of his father, who was Acting Fiscal in the Cape at the time (Hewett 1998: xiii), Hemmy's Leiden dissertation (1770), also in Latin, deals with the 'validity' of testimony given at legal hearings by Indians, Chinese and other 'pagan peoples' in the East Indies, and by the Hottentots at the Cape, revealing, as Varley says, that 'he already had thoughts of Company service, possibly in the East' (White 1959: iv). He indeed entered the service of the Company and served in the Indies and Japan, where he died (Hewett 1998: xvi-xvii).

Roman-Dutch law of the period regarded certain groups and individuals as unworthy or incapable of testifying in a court of law – among these were slaves, the insane, prostitutes, heretics, Jews (in cases against 'orthodox' Christians), Jesuits and bishops (van Stekelenburg 2003: 105). It is thus unsurprising that Hemmy, whose father was a public prosecutor at the time, should tackle the question whether or not the testimony of 'pagan peoples', who fell within the Dutch East India

Company's sphere of influence, should be valid in Dutch courts of law. As he revealed in his attitude to the Hottentots in his *oratio*, Hemmy assumes a positive attitude towards these 'native peoples' on moral grounds tinged with characteristically Dutch expediency: how can we trade with these people and then regard their evidence in law-courts on the same level as that of heretics? Not to speak of Jews and heretical bishops. These 'pagan peoples' should therefore not be regarded as *intestabiles* (incapable of giving evidence in a court of law).

His father had made a particular request that his dissertation should deal with the Hottentots and their testimony (Hewett 1998: 59). In the final section, therefore, Hemmy dutifully carries out his father's wishes, echoing the positive account of the Hottentots he had given in his earlier *oratio*. Acknowledging that the Hottentots are pagans and that some are probably unworthy of giving evidence in a law court, he argues that this is the fault of their environment and socialization. In a remarkable passage, redolent with the environmental determinism which characterized Enlightenment thinking, he writes:

> ... for if, perhaps, that most brilliant of English philosophers, the great Newton had been born in Saldanha Bay, his thoughts, I am sure, would not have differed much from the Hottentots living there and, on the other hand, if by chance some Hottentot had at that time been born in England, he would perhaps have left the men learned in the science of mathematics, philosophy and astronomy many parasangs behind him (quoted in Hewett 1998: 62).

Thus he concludes that the Hottentots, certainly those of unblemished reputation living among Christians at the Cape, 'must not be deprived of the right of giving testimony in Court' (ibid.: 63).

What is interesting about both Hemmy's oration and the topic of his dissertation is that he engages, in his academic researches, with his country of origin and with other cultures which were in the orbit of the Dutch East India Company – very different from the work of the Afrikaans-speaking scholars who sailed to the Netherlands in the twentieth century, work which is narrowly specialized and does not engage, with the exception of Haarhoff, with South Africa and its peoples. Hemmy's classical education in Germany and the Netherlands is, despite or perhaps because of its mercenary purposes, politically *engagé*.

Furthermore on the title page of his *oratio* he identifies himself as '*Afer*' (African) and on that of his dissertation as '*Promontorio Bonae Spei Batavus*' (a Dutchman from the Cape of Good Hope), thus perceiving himself as an African Dutchman, apparently comfortable with his dual identities and, for a born-and-bred Cape settler, remarkably free of racial prejudice.

In contrast, the work of his intellectual descendants strikes one as unengaged. However, by choosing not to engage with South Africa and its cultures, or by focusing on ethical issues, such as the ethics of Seneca and Calvin, which have especial relevance to the Dutch Reformed Church, their work, in the South African context, becomes politically charged and positions itself within the ideology of the ruling élite.[16]

The Classics, the British and Afrikaner identity in the Cape

In fact, the fate of the study of Classics at the Cape, as will be argued throughout this book, is inextricably bound up with political change and the quest for Afrikaner identity, which generally characterizes the history of education in South Africa.[17] After the first British occupation (1795-1803), a brief Dutch interregnum, the second British occupation in 1806 and the formal annexation of the Cape in 1815, the Anglicization of the Cape began – a process which became increasingly aggressive as the immigration of British settlers to the Cape increased and the Colony became more urbanized (Davenport 1991: 35-41).

The second 'Latin school', which had an unimpressive eight pupils in 1809 (Behr 1952: 206), was transformed into an English grammar school with an English rector (the Reverend E.C. Judge, a classicist) (Smuts 1960: 8; Behr 1952: 156) and so began the tension between the Dutch settler families and the English colonizers over the language of education and the accessibility of public schools to all races, prominent features of the history of education in South Africa during the nineteenth and twentieth centuries.

When English was made the official language of the Cape Colony in 1822 (Smuts 1960: 8), educated members of the Dutch-speaking white population began to establish private schools, in which Dutch was the medium of education. One such school was the appropriately-named Riebeeks Instituut which offered Latin, Greek and Hebrew, essential for study for the ministry in the Netherlands (ibid.: 8); the founders of the school, Faure and Berrangé, were both churchmen with strong academic links with the Netherlands.[18]

However, even before this, Cradock's reforms of public education at the Cape (1813) which, influenced by British models, introduced free schools for the poor, open to blacks, provided some members of the Dutch settler community with more pressing reasons for establishing private schools, if not for leaving the Cape altogether.[19] The radical Ordinance 50 of 1828, which made all races equal before the law,[20] even before the abolition of slavery throughout the British Empire (1833) and the gradual freeing of slaves at the Cape (1834-1838),[21] simply added to the anxieties of many of the Dutch settlers. Karel Trichardt, one of the leaders of the Great Trek (c. 1835-1838), that exodus of white Dutch settlers and their black servants from the Eastern Cape in pursuit of a life in the Transvaal, Orange Free State and Natal, free from what was perceived as perfidious British neglect, gave as the main reason for the Trek *'de gelijkstelling van kleurlingen met de blanken'* (the equality of coloureds with whites).[22] *'Gelijkstelling'* was, of course, not the sole reason: to this must be added land, labour and security problems, 'which they [the Boers] felt unable to address due to a lack of representation, giving rise to a profound sense of marginalization' (Giliomee and Mbenga 2008: 108).

Political marginalization was inextricably linked to the language issue. Initially, the British authorities were not completely insensitive. When, in 1829, South Africa's first institute of higher learning (the Athenaeum or South African College) was established, with the help of the Dutch Reformed Church (Giliomee 2008: 96), the Reverend Judge, the Rector of the English-speaking grammar school, which was incorporated into the College, became the first English professor of Classics, and the Reverend Faure taught Classics in Dutch (ibid.: 9), thus initiating parallel-medium education, for so long a feature of many white South African state schools, in keeping with the later ideology of *apartheid* or ethnic separation.[23]

Without the long tradition of classical scholarship which anchored the curriculum in English, Scottish and Dutch universities (these being the three traditions most pertinent to the development of education in South Africa), no colonial university founded in a multi-cultural society in the nineteenth century could survive by focusing largely on a classical

32

curriculum.[24] Under the Dutch, the Cape was nothing more (from a European perspective, that is) than the veritable 'last outpost' of a company in terminal decline. However, with the arrival of the British, the Cape Colony became 'linked to the most developed, dynamic industrial country in the world' (Tamarkin 1996: 17). Not only did this profoundly affect the Cape economy, but it also had lasting political, social and educational repercussions.

Ten years after the foundation of the South African College, Herschel's educational reforms – which introduced other subjects, such as Natural History and Physical Science, into the curriculum – were implemented in the College, and a school system was instituted in which elementary schools would offer education in Dutch or English and high schools would offer the Classics in English only.[25] This was a radically discriminatory move, typical of subsequent South African education, where language was used as a potent political weapon to exclude the dominated from the governing class. A knowledge of the Classics still qualified one for entrance into the bureaucratic, political and social élites of the then burgeoning British empire (Smuts 1960: 12-13). As Francois Smuts modestly comments: the Herschel reform was 'responsible for a certain alienation of the Afrikaans-speaking group from the Classics' (ibid.: 13) and, it should be added, from the centres of power, which fact was not forgotten by Afrikaans-speaking educationalists and classicists in subsequent years.

In keeping with the Anglicization of the Cape and the intellectual imperialism attendant upon it, a parade of graduates from Oxford, London and Cambridge dominated the Classics and education in the Cape from the middle until the end of the nineteenth century.[26] In 1918, the University of the Cape of Good Hope became the University of South Africa, and the South African College and Victoria College (in Stellenbosch) became independent universities (ibid.: 16) – the University of Cape Town and the University of Stellenbosch. For our argument, it is important, briefly, to look at features in the history of the latter institution.

The phenomenal growth of the Dutch Reformed Church in the Cape Colony in the first half of the nineteenth century should not be ignored in any analysis of the growth of Afrikaner identity on social, cultural and intellectual levels (Tamarkin 1996: 31). In contrast to the Dutch East India Company, which protected the Dutch Reformed Church's monopoly on Christianity, the British introduced religious pluralism, which effectively thrust the DRC into the competitive market-place for souls – white and black (Giliomee and Mbenga 2008: 95-101). Hence the establishment of a seminary in Stellenbosch in 1859 to train ministers for the Reformed congregations, established in almost fifty towns and villages by 1854, which served as a catalyst for the development of education in the classical languages in the town.

In his speech at the opening of the seminary, the Reverend Professor Murray, a Scot who had studied Theology in the Netherlands, defends the study of the classical languages, not simply as necessary for the study of the Bible, but also for the intellectual training and discipline they impart, a familiar nineteenth-century argument, still employed today by many South African universities anxious to defend the study of the Classics in Africa. Interestingly, Murray declares that 'we shall strive to imprint the old Netherlands stamp on our teaching', and this in a context in which English educational officials were striving, if anything, to imprint the old Oxbridge stamp 'on our teaching'. Murray and two theological allies joined forces and proposed the establishment of a gymnasium in the town which would give students, *inter alia*, 'a thorough training in the subjects which are counted as a civilized education' (Smuts 1960: 24) and prepare them for entrance into the seminary. Yet another ordained Scot, the Reverend Baird – the austere Calvinism of the Scots appealed more to the Dutch Reformed Church than the neo-Papist rituals of High Anglicanism – was appointed rector of the gymnasium when it opened in 1866, and eight years later a fellow countryman, Macdonald, occupied the first chair of English and Classics (ibid.: 24). This phalanx of Scots (more were to come) meant that the language of instruction for most classes was English; this combined with the triumphalist re-naming of the college as Victoria College in 1887, which, despite being celebrated by many Afrikaner politicians and intellectuals at the time, may well have contributed to the flowering of Afrikaner nationalism at Stellenbosch, particularly after the betrayal of Afrikaner trust by Cecil Rhodes when he was Premier of the Colony (see Chapter 2).

Predictably, in the wake of this betrayal and the South African War (1899-1902), the language in which the Classics was imparted became the focus of nationalistic aspirations at Stellenbosch. Van Braam, born in the Netherlands and a graduate of the University of Utrecht, had been professor of Latin at Rhodes University College in Grahamstown, before he moved to Classics at Stellenbosch (1913-1946) where he introduced Afrikaans as the medium of instruction (ibid.:28).[27] On this important move, Smuts, one of von Braam's successors in the Chair of Latin, comments:

> This was a salutary principle, as almost unconsciously the fact of studying a subject from the elementary stages up to University level through another language than the mother-tongue, although it brought many advantages, set a certain distance between student and subject matter. This was aggravated, of course, by the fact that the Afrikaans-speaking section had also been partly alienated from the academic ideals of their Dutch forefathers in the process of their long isolation in Southern Africa. They had to build up a new academic tradition for themselves, of which Classical scholarship was to form an integral part (ibid.: 28-9).

Smuts' earnest commitment to a 'new academic tradition', which obviously involved the translation of major classical works into Afrikaans, for which the Classics Department at Stellenbosch is very well known,[28] and thus the popularization of the Classics amongst the 'Afrikaans-speaking section', is here combined with the elegiac yearning for the 'academic ideals of their Dutch forefathers'. Considering that most of the students at Stellenbosch at this period would have been from religious backgrounds in rural farming communities, where, it must be admitted, good schools which taught Latin did exist (ibid.: 25), and descendants of *burgher* rather than intellectual forefathers, the 'academic ideals of their Dutch forefathers' sounds like an example of the mythologizing of ancestry, often encountered in the colonized whose language has been suppressed and who thus feel the need to forge a distinct identity. Building up 'a new academic tradition for themselves', rooted in the translation and thus appropriation of the Classics, became an important feature of the intellectual formation of Cape Afrikaner identity. Smuts may have had in mind Murray's 'the old Netherlands stamp on our teaching', but his reference to the 'process of their long isolation in Southern Africa' suggests the loneliness of the *Afrikaner* under British rule, severed from his roots, forging, reluctantly, a new civilization and identity on the tip of Africa.

When Francois Smuts was a student at Stellenbosch in the years before the Second World War (Conradie 1987: 1), the battle for the official recognition of Afrikaans had almost been won, but it was a battle which had left its wounds and scars. Charting shifts in power, Dutch (even though Afrikaans was by now widely spoken) and English jostled for supremacy in South African schools in the late nineteenth and early twentieth centuries. In the Transvaal Republic in 1882, Dutch was the medium of instruction (Behr and Macmillan 1966: 104-5); after the defeat of the Boers in the South African War (1899-1902), Lord Milner reversed the policy and made English the language of instruction (ibid.: 107). In the Orange Free State before the war, Dutch was the medium of instruction in all rural schools and English or Dutch in urban schools; after the war, English (ibid.: 121-3). The Smuts Act of 1907 made it obligatory for every child to learn English, although some provision for Dutch was made, particularly in religious education. After the Union of South Africa (1910), this Act was amended to give English and Dutch equal status, and was extended to Afrikaans in 1914 (ibid.: 109-10). In 1923 Afrikaans was introduced in Natal schools (ibid.: 119), two years before it became an official parliamentary language.

As we have already seen, legislation had ensured that English was the medium of instruction in Cape schools throughout the latter half of the nineteenth century. Not all Afrikaners disapproved of this; in fact there is evidence that many families wanted their children to receive an education in English rather than Dutch. As Tamarkin notes:

> the anglicized education system provided emerging generations of educated Afrikaners with a linguistic tool which facilitated their integration into the steadily expanding bureaucracy (1996: 30).

Thus an important reason for learning English was that it provided a tool for Afrikaner *political* advancement. When the Cape Colony was granted Representative Government with a bicameral parliament in 1853, English was the sole parliamentary language, which obviously acted as a check on Afrikaner political participation in debates in the colonial parliament. Furthermore, on the granting of Responsible Government in 1872 and control of the colony's finances, which directly impinged on the daily lives, needs and problems of white Afrikaner farmers, the need to learn English, which was still the only permissible parliamentary language, became even more urgent. A decade later, Afrikaner politicians won the right to use Dutch in parliament, aided by Hofmeyr, the Afrikaner Bond and the crucial support of Rhodes (see Chapter 2).

Although the granting of Responsible Government in 1872 increased the importance of English as the language of power, it also aroused Dutch and Afrikaans-speaking farmers from their notorious political apathy and created a space for identity politics, as the fight to use Dutch in the Cape parliament demonstrates. Giliomee and others have rightly argued that nationalism often develops in tandem with industrialization, access to the wealth it brings and the 'class cleavages' which capitalism creates (1987: 28-41).

In the predominantly agricultural economy of the Cape before 1870, Dutch or Afrikaans speakers did not need education for an urban market-place. However, after the discovery of diamonds (1867), the annexation of the diamond fields by Britain (1871) and the rapid industrialization of the Cape economy, education began to assume a critical importance, evident in the growth of the number of schools (for whites) in the Cape in the latter half of the nineteenth century (Giliomee 1987: 60). A growth in the number of schools necessitated a rise in the number of teachers, not only of English, but also of Dutch and, eventually, Afrikaans: it is among these teachers and lecturers at university colleges (such as von Braam) that we find, what Smith and Seton-Watson deem the 'secular intellectuals' or 'language manipulators' (in Giliomee 1987: 30, 60), who helped create a sense of national Afrikaner identity, especially in the years after the South African War (1899-1902). A good example of a cultural association involved in creating this sense of national identity was the Afrikaans-Hollandse Toneelvereniging (Afrikaans-Dutch Drama Association), established in Pretoria in 1907, committed to the performance of plays in Afrikaans, in particular translations of the classical repertoire (Euripides' *Medea* was the choice for 1908): notably, productions by the AHTV were usually preceded by the singing of '*Afrikanders Bo!*' ('Afikaners On Top!') to the tune of the Netherlands national anthem – in direct opposition to the colonial power's 'God Save the King!' (van Zyl Smit 2007: 74).

However, in the 1870s upward political and social mobility, by exploiting alliances with imperialist Britain and its capitalist agents, seemed to many to be more important than linguistic identity, although the struggle for the right to use the *'moedertaal'* (the 'mother language') in parliament began to crystallize ideas of Afrikaans nationalism and identity, especially in the popular press where there were clearly attempts to define what 'Afrikaner' actually meant (Giliomee 1987: 35-6). It is not unsurprising that the advent of Responsible Government and the struggle for Afrikaner political representation should be inextricably linked to the struggle for the recognition of Afrikaans in its competition with English and Dutch.

As a spoken language distinct from Dutch, Afrikaans, according to the classicist Haarhoff, had been identifiable since 1750 (1934: 15); however, Haarhoff romanticizes the origins of the language and ignores its black, servile, creole and non-Christian roots (Shell 1994: 61-4). Giliomee has suggested that 'by the end of the seventeenth century Cape Dutch had largely become what is now Afrikaans' (2008: 71). In the latter half of the nineteenth century Afrikaans was considered the language of the poor white class and the 'coloured' Muslim community in the Cape, many of whom were descendants of freed slaves (Giliomee 1987: 39-40). Employing Arabic script, Cape Muslims were the first community (*c.* 1856) to print texts in Afrikaans; furthermore, Afrikaans was the language used in Muslim schools (Giliomee and Mbenga 2008: 71, 101).

Associating the identifying term 'Afrikaner' with the white community who spoke Afrikaans illustrates, most aptly, how the processes of identification are inextricably linked to power and the appropriation of language. It was the British who called the offspring of white settlers and slaves 'Afrikanders' (or Afrikaners) (Giliomee and Mbenga 2008: 53), although there is evidence, as early as 1707, of a white settler, of German and Dutch descent, referring to himself as an 'Africaander' (ibid.: 62). As early as 1830, the first Dutch newspaper (*De Zuid-Afrikaan*) – no newspapers were produced during the Dutch occupation of the Cape – used the term 'Afrikaner' (positively) for all colonists (ibid.: 96). In the latter half of the nineteenth century, however, after decades of British rule, the process of appropriating this identity and investing it with positive connotations was inchoate: many upper-class, educated Afrikaners still preferred using English or Dutch and were opposed to the use of Afrikaans, especially in public, as it was the language of the 'uncivilized' (ibid.: 41-2). Tamarkin notes that even

Hofmeyr (as late as 1875) addressed a meeting at Stellenbosch in English (1996: 30).

The battle for the recognition of Afrikaans as a language with an identity separate from Dutch, would not have been achieved without the formation, in 1875, of the Genootskap van Regte Afrikaners (Association of True Afrikaners), which included among its ranks a Dutch teacher of classical languages at the Paarl Gymnasium (Arnoldus Pannevis), whose student, S.J. du Toit, a descendant of Huguenot settlers, was elected President of the Association.[29] Pannevis, who had first suggested the establishment of the Genootskap, recommended du Toit as translator of the Bible into Afrikaans, precisely because of his knowledge of Hebrew and ancient Greek (ibid.: 47). The importance of the classical tradition and the formative years of Afrikaner identity struggles in the Cape should not be overlooked.[30]

According to the minutes of the Association's meetings held in Paarl (1875-1878), this significant alliance of clergymen, teachers of the classical languages and wine farmers formed the Association '*om te staan vir ons Taal, ons Nasie en ons Land*' (to stand for our Language, our Nation and our Land) (Article II of the constitution, Nienaber 1974: 53). What was perceived as the language of the poorer 'coloured' and ex-slave classes was now being appropriated and owned by members of the white educated and commercial class, for 'our Language' clearly meant Afrikaans, not Dutch. Furthermore the Association also made explicit links between religious identity and a secretive nationalism, reactive to possible hostility from both the British and other Afrikaners loyal to Dutch.[31]

To convince all Afrikaners that Afrikaans (not Dutch) was in fact their language, and to standardize the language, the Association decided that its first task was to publish a monthly newspaper, *Die Afrikaanse Patriot*, an Afrikaans dictionary, and school textbooks, including an Afrikaans grammar (Articles XII, XIV; Nienaber 1974: 54). The first meeting also approved motions to circulate the '*Afrikaanse Volkslied*' (Afrikaans People's Anthem) and translate the Bible into Afrikaans (ibid.: 1-2) – crucially important to the Genootskap's strategy. The '*lied*', composed by Pannevis, Hoogenhout, S.J. du Toit and D.F. du Toit, reveals what the Genootskap considered were the essential building-blocks of an ethnic nationalism and identity: land, language, religion, law, justice and time – the latter in the sense of 'every *volk* has its time' (Geldenhuys 1967: 13-14). For the Genootskap, the Afrikaners' god-ordained time was at hand.

In the first edition of the newspaper, which appeared in January 1876, a stirring manifesto opened with a carefully-annotated biblical justification for the right to speak one's own *god-given* language. In contrast to the rulers Ahasuerus and Mithridates, who had permitted conquered peoples in their domain to use their own languages, the British, argued the manifesto, had imposed English on 'OUR Parliament', 'OUR Courts' and 'OUR Schools (Nienaber 1974: 59-60). Furthermore they had no respect for 'Hollans', which was demoted to the level of a 'Kaffertaal' (ibid.: 60). Using Wales, Poland, Flanders, Friesland and Ireland as examples of places where *'die moedertaal'* (the mother-tongue) had survived, despite the efforts of conquerors to suppress it, the writer of the manifesto concluded by boasting that Afrikaans had also survived and was growing:

> Die grootste gros van ons natie praat almal nog Afrikaans. Mar daar is daarom drie soorte van Afrikaanders ... Daar is *Afrikaanders met* ENGELSE *harte*. En daar is *Afrikaanders met* HOLLANSE *harte*. En dan is daar *Afrikaanders met* AFRIKAANSE HARTE. Die laaste noem ons REGTE AFRIKAANDERS, en die veral roep ons op om an ons kant te kom staan.

> (The largest majority of our nation all speak Afrikaans. But there are thus three kinds of Afrikaanders ... There are *Afrikaanders with* ENGLISH *hearts*. And there are *Afrikaanders with* DUTCH *hearts*. And then there are *Afrikaanders with* AFRIKAANS HEARTS. These we name TRUE AFRIKAANDERS, and these we especially call upon to come and stand at our side) (quoted in Nienaber 1974: 61).

With these words, the writer clarifies what the Genootskap understood by *'ons Nasie'* (our Nation) and delineates the nature of the 'class cleavages' among Afrikaners themselves. *'Regte Afrikaanders'* (true Afrikaners) are neither those, in the colonial bureaucracy and capitalist enterprises, who had sold out to British imperialism and the English language, nor those, in intellectual and clerical circles, who fostered ties

40

with the Netherlands and promoted 'High Dutch', but those whose identities were unambiguously rooted in South Africa and who embraced the cause of Afrikaans.

Letters of resignation from the Genootskap confirm that the Dutch Reformed Church was putting pressure on its students in its seminaries to master Dutch, which was the language of the Bible and church services (Nienaber 1974: 65-6). On behalf of the Association, a reply to a schoolteacher from 'Lokomotief', written at about the same time as the Manifesto, reiterates the Genootskap's position: it is impossible to make a Dutchman out of an 'Afrikaander' with an Afrikaans heart (ibid.: 67). 'Lokomotief''s impassioned article in *Die Afrikaanse Patriot* of 1877 employs militaristic language to confirm that 'our most poisonous enemies' are fellow Afrikaners, whilst there are many '*ordentlike Engelse*' (respectable Englishmen) who 'endorse our cause and support it' (ibid.: 78).

To get some idea of what the not so '*ordentlike Engelse*' thought of Afrikaners and Afrikaans, a sneering editorial in the *Cape Times*, representative of extreme jingoism, dismissed the term 'Afrikaner' as a name originally applied 'to the half-bred off-spring of slaves and even in a word the mark of slavery is detestable' (Giliomee 1987: 36). Embedded in these paternalistic prejudices was an undeniable fact: Bird records, in 1822, that the term 'Afrikander' was used at the Cape of creole slaves, in contrast to Negro and Malay slaves (in Shell 1994: 56). Similar prejudices about the nature of the creole *patois* were obviously held in the metropolis. Pannevis' request (1875), on behalf of the Genootskap, to print a Bible in Cape Dutch (i.e. Afrikaans) prompted the following response from the British & Foreign Bible Society in London:

> We are by no means inclined to perpetuate jargons by printing Scriptures in them, & nothing but the most undoubted information that there are a large number of *readers* who use this dialect & who cannot make use of either the English or Dutch Bible would justify us in printing it (quoted in Nienaber 1974: 47).

Important political and economic developments in the 1870s also contributed to the promotion of Afrikaans and the forging of an Afrikaner identity in the Cape, despite the 'class cleavages' referred to above. In 1878, in reaction to the severe setbacks suffered by wine, wheat and wool farmers (Giliomee 1987: 55-8), Jan Hofmeyr established the Zuid-afrikaanse Boeren Beschermings Vereniging (Association for the Protection of South African farmers), and S.J. du Toit, the erstwhile President of the Genootskap, the Afrikaner Bond in 1880. The Associations merged to become the new Afrikaner Bond in 1883, which developed into a significant force in Cape politics (Giliomee 1987: 37-9).[32]

Precisely because of the fact that Pannevis, S.J. du Toit and others had originally chosen to fight the campaign for Afrikaans and Afrikaner identity on the literary and cultural plain, the public schools and teacher training colleges – where, complained the *Zuid Afrikaan* in 1890, almost all the teachers were English or Scottish 'or South Africans with a limited knowledge of Dutch' (Tamarkin 1996: 29) – became the battlegrounds for a reactive nationalism, centred on language rights. To the schools and colleges should be added (eventually) the Dutch Reformed Church and the Afrikaans press, which contributed enormously to the raising of the status of Afrikaans and the obsolescence of Dutch.[33]

Haarhoff, distinguished Afrikaans-speaking classicist, educated at the South African College, Berlin and Oxford, notes, with some bitterness, that when he attended the South African College School in Cape Town in the early twentieth century, he was taught 'to be ashamed of his own language, which was dealt with in a perfunctory way and inspected by a man who could not pronounce it' (1934: 29). Such experiences, not atypical of many educated Afrikaners in the Cape during this period, obviously contributed to the rise of Afrikaner nationalism in the educated classes which had originally resisted the use of Afrikaans.

Such is the background to the generation of Afrikaans-speaking classicists who, having been educated in a context reactive to that which shaped Haarhoff's resentment, established the Classical Association of South Africa. In 1956, when the Association was formed with Francois Smuts as a founder member, the Union of South Africa – a self-governing state within the British Empire – was still a member of the Commonwealth, and English and Afrikaans were the two official languages. African languages were ignored. Under the ruling Nationalist Party, which had won the elections in 1948, the legislative path had been cleared for the entrenchment of the policy of *apartheid*, or separate development, largely through the efforts of Dr H. Verwoerd, the Minister of Native Affairs and the country's Prime Minister from 1958 until his assassination in 1966.[34]

Important legislation passed before 1956 which obviously affected education and thus the position of Classics in South Africa included the Bantu Education Act of 1953, which legislated a system of education which separated the kind of education and training available to whites and blacks (or non-whites or Bantu) and the institutions in which this could take place (Behr and Macmillan 1966: 348-51). A year after this (1954), in order to carry out these policies, the control of 'Bantu education' was transferred from the provincial administrations and the churches to the Department of Native Affairs in the central government. In the same year, Verwoerd made his now notorious speech in which he declared that there was no place for the African in European society above certain levels of labour (Hepple 1967: 125), a belief which revealed his innate conviction in the intellectual inferiority of African peoples and underpinned the policies of separate development, Bantu education and the construction of white-owned factories near pools of cheap black labour. This legislation would effectively sound the death knell of the mission schools, as these schools would have to pass into the control of the department and the academic freedom to teach what and how they wished would be severely curtailed.

Threats of school boycotts and protest meetings greeted news of this legislation. In June 1955 the Congress of the People met and the Freedom Charter, which forms the basis of the political beliefs of the African National Congress, was presented in Kliptown, Soweto, on the 25/26 June 1955 (Davenport 1991: 350-1). The Freedom Charter Campaign, which had been initiated by the ANC in 1954 and was intended to prepare a constitution for a 'democratic, unified and non-racial South Africa' (Chipkin 2007: 65) was obviously very threatening to the Afrikaner nationalist government and its supporters, particularly as some of its clauses revealed the influence of the very Communist ideology which the Suppression of Communism Act (1950) had been deployed to obviate (ibid.: 67-82). Furthermore, the clauses referring to education were an unequivocal rejection of the racist separatism legislated by the Bantu Education Act. Under the section headed 'The Doors of Learning and Culture Shall be Opened!' were statements such as these:

'Education shall be free, compulsory, universal and equal for all children. ... The colour bar in cultural life, in sport and in education shall be abolished (Freedom Charter, 1955).

1956 was the year in which 'coloured' voters were disenfranchised by an act of unscrupulous gerrymandering (Davenport 1991: 343). In the same year, four months after the Classical Association was founded in Pretoria, the now legendary women's protest march against the extension of the Pass Laws to women took place at the Union Buildings in the capital city (ibid.: 348). 1956 was also the year in which the Treason Trials (1956-1961), during which South Africans of all races were indicted and tried under the Suppression of Communism Act, began (ibid.: 351-2).

These were the turbulent political times during which the Classical Association as it is now constituted was formed. Just as not all German classicists in the 1930s were supporters of Hitler or Spanish scholars *franquistas*, it is simply inaccurate to suggest that all Afrikaans-speaking classicists who formed CASA were supporters of Verwoerd – Haarhoff, one of the first Honorary Presidents of the Association, certainly wasn't (Whitaker 1997: 7, 11). Furthermore it is equally naïve to believe that, as classicists, they were immune to the inhumane policies pursued by their elected government and the brutality with which these were implemented. In addition, the groves of academe had provided the theoreticians of *apartheid*. Verwoerd himself had been a professor of Sociology at the University of Stellenbosch; van Eiselen, his Secretary of Native Affairs, a classicist turned anthropologist from the same university (Smuts 1960: 29); during these years Verwoerd and other academics formed the backbone of the Afrikaner Broederbond, an Afrikaner secret society dedicated to the aggressive promotion of Afrikaner nationalism, Christian nationalist beliefs and Afrikaans in every sector of South African society (Davenport 1991: 290). Significant organizations within the Broederbond network included the Instituut vir Christelik Nasionale Onderwys (Institute for Christian National Education) and the Federasie vir Afrikaanse Kultuurverenigings (Federation for Afrikaner Cultural Associations), which worked closely together to forge a master plan for the implementation of Christian National Education, which became the prevailing educational philosophy in the state school system (Hepple 1967: 68; Bloomberg 1990: 56).

Verwoerd fervently believed that the very future of South Africa was threatened if every child (presumably white child) was not educated as a 'patriotic person' (Hepple 1967: 232).

CASA and the promotion of Afrikaans

One thought which must have been uppermost in the minds of most of the academics who formed the Classical Association in 1956, many of whom had been educated at Stellenbosch and other Afrikaans-speaking universities during the years when the struggle for the recognition of Afrikaans was especially acute,[35] was the promotion of Afrikaans as an academic language and, in particular, as a language into which the admired classics of Greece and Rome had to be translated. As Smuts was to remark later (1976: 20), '... *geen volk kan die Klassieke volkome sy eie maak sonder vertalings in die volkstaal nie*' (no people can make the Classics completely their own without translations into the language of the people). As a Cape Afrikaner, Smuts's use of '*volk*' and '*volkstaal*' situates him directly in the tradition of the fight for the '*moedertaal*' which characterized the burgeoning of Afrikaner ethnic identity in the Cape in the late nineteenth century (Tamarkin 1996: 180, 274).

Afrikaans had been recognized as an official language for use in the schools in 1914, but only in 1925 did it replace Dutch as one of the official parliamentary languages (along with English). The year before this Verwoerd had written his doctoral thesis in psychology in Afrikaans at the University of Stellenbosch – 'the first of its kind to be written in Afrikaans', notes Hepple (1967: 20). Many of the founding *patres* had written their theses in Afrikaans too; hence their preference for post-graduate study at universities in the Netherlands.[36]

In the 1950s Afrikaans was still a young language which required aggressive promotion in both schools and universities if it was to survive and flourish after decades of domination by English as the language of public policy and instruction. Haarhoff himself, together with van den Heever, had written a passionate monograph entitled *The Achievement of Afrikaans*, pleading with intolerant English speakers for the acceptance of Afrikaans as a language with a vibrant literature and a muscular energy, making it far more suitable for translation of the Homeric epics than English. Strikingly, the book was dedicated to

45

the Spirit of Racial Understanding (between English and Afrikaans-speaking South Africans), yet proceeds from the sale of the book were 'to strengthen the funds for the Voortrekker Monument' (Haarhoof 1934: v), an iconic focus of aggressive Afrikaner nationalism at the time, with suggestive architectural links to the fascist architecture of both Hitler and Mussolini (*pace* Evans 2007: 154).

H.L. Gonin, the first chairman of the Association, and a direct descendant of the Dutch Reformed Church missionary, Henri Gonin (Giliomee and Mbenga 2008: 153), acutely aware that Afrikaans-speaking students had to study Latin through the medium of English text books and commentaries, had published, even before the first conference, his graded *Latynse Grammatika en Leesboek* (Latin Grammar and Reader, 1944, 1945, 1947). In a 75th birthday tribute to Gonin, published in *Acta Classica*, Smuts, writing in Afrikaans, hailed the publication of this grammar (and Gonin's later works for high school students) as empowering the Afrikaans-speaker to study the Classics in his mother-tongue, which it was hoped would result in more enthusiasm for the study of the Classics among Afrikaners (1981: xii). Smuts goes on to comment on the significance of the fact that the revival of the Classical Association in 1956 was led by a number of young scholars, former students and colleagues of Gonin (ibid.), who clearly believed fervently in the promotion of Afrikaans as an academic language. Smuts also notes that many of the first Greek and Latin textbooks were produced by former students of van Braam at Stellenbosch – the Dutch Latinist who had been the first at that university to give his Latin classes in Afrikaans (1976: 13).

Significantly, all the papers at the first conference at which the association was formed, with the exception of one, were given in Afrikaans, although the principle of bilingualism was enshrined in the constitution of the association.[37] Furthermore, at the second conference at Stellenbosch (1957) a committee was elected to 'consult with the Suid-Afrikaanse Akademie on the spelling of Greek proper nouns in Afrikaans'.[38] The Akademie then established formal links with CASA through its Taalkommissie (Language Commission), a committee driven by fanatical Afrikaner nationalism.[39]

CASA's concern to protect and promote Afrikaans is also revealed in the debate over the publication of the proceedings of the first conference as a *Festschrift* in honour of Professor Haarhoff, the doyen of South

African classicists, who had recently retired. One of the objections raised to the use of Blackwell's as a publisher (who were willing to publish the collection of papers provided that the collection was accessible to an English-speaking readership) was the obvious fact that papers written in Afrikaans would have to be excluded and, in addition, Haarhoff's work had 'propagated the fusion of Classical and Afrikaner culture' (Henderson 2004: 95). This volume was eventually published by the publishing company Balkema in 1959 as volume one of *Acta Classica*, CASA's official journal; of the sixteen academic papers in the first volume, only two are written in Afrikaans (by Smuts and van Rooy, both of whom were present at the foundation meeting).[40] Balkema itself was a Dutch company with a branch in Cape Town, committed to the publication of Africana and academic works written in Afrikaans. Another objection to the publication of the papers by Blackwell's in Oxford was the fear that foreign contributors would outnumber local ones.[41]

Romans and Boers

In place of the abandoned *Festschrift*, the first volume of *Acta Classica* was presented to Professor Haarhoff at the third conference in Bloemfontein in 1959. In his fulsome *laudatio* on this occasion, Professor Steven, speaking in both English and Afrikaans and peppering his speech with Greek and Latin allusions, referred to the parallels Haarhoff made in his work between the early Roman farmer and the Voortrekker – 'between the *anima naturaliter stoica* and the *anima naturaliter Calviniana*' (Henderson 2004: 101), the soul which is by nature Stoic and that which is by nature Calvinist. Interestingly, Haarhoff's analogy focuses on the moral character of the Voortrekker, who loomed large in Afrikaner mythology and in nationalist iconography: in 1938 the centenary of the Great Trek had been celebrated in Pretoria and the Voortrekker monument had been built to commemorate this event. In Bloemfontein, where the volume was presented, was the 'Vrouemonument' (Women's Monument) which remembered the thousands of Afrikaner women and children who had died in British concentration camps during the South African War (1899-1902). Haarhoff had thus seized on a powerful symbol of Afrikaner nationalism and resistance to British imperialism, which must have had especially potent resonances during the early years of Nationalist Party rule and

Verwoerd's rise to power. Yet Stevens is at pains to distance Haarhoff from any exclusive political ideology by emphasizing his inclusive *humanitas*: his political ideal is a united people where Afrikaner and Englishman, German and Frenchman can work together for the benefit of '*ons land Suid-Afrika*' (our land South Africa).

The deliberate grouping together of white South Africans and their white immigrant Protestant ancestors, the complete omission of any reference to the black majority, the echo of Langenhoven's poem, at this stage the national anthem,[42] the emotive use of words such as '*vaderlandsliewend*' (fatherland-loving), the reference to a Karoo farmer (*Karoo-boer*) who found Haarhoff's *Die Romeinse Boer* (The Roman Farmer, Haarhoff's version of Vergil's *Georgics* in Afrikaans) the best handbook on farming (*boerdery*) he had ever read, all situate the orator (and Haarhoff, despite his inclusive *humanitas*) within the political ideology of white South Africa and the ruling Afrikaner elite.

Haarhoff's reply in Latin is especially interesting. He tactfully mentions Lubbe, the secretary, *honoris causa*, and Professor Petrie who, together with Haarhoff, had been elected Honorary Presidents of the Classical Association at its first meeting in Pretoria (Henderson 2004: 90). A Scot, educated at Aberdeen and Cambridge, Petrie had been a founding member of the earlier Classical Association established in 1927 in Cape Town (ibid. 2004: 90 n. 4). The mention of Lubbe, as representative of the 'new' generation of Afrikaans-speaking classicists, and Petrie ('*Nestor sane noster sapientissimus*'), the colossus of English-speaking classicists, who had established the Department of Classics at the University of Natal in 1910, suggests the kind of inclusiveness, the embracing of *Boer* and *Brit* (and thankfully a Scot!) for which Haarhoff was well known. At the end of his speech, Haarhoff's final flourish, after a citation from Vergil's *Georgics*, is also intriguing: '*Floreat, vivat, in hoc tam barbaro mundo societas nostra classica Africae Australis*' (May our Classical Association of South Africa flourish and prosper in so barbarous a world as this).What did Haarhoff mean by '*in hoc tam barbaro mundo*'? The world at large? The all white, predominantly Afrikaans-speaking, Classical Association as a cultural beacon in a sea of black barbarism? I suspect the latter. Haarhoff's deep love for Vergil – his annual Vergil lectures commemorating Vergil's birthday were much-loved cultural events in Johannesburg, enlivened by some spiritualist eccentricities, such as leaving a vacant chair for the spirit of Vergil with whom he was in regular communication[43] – extended to the *pax Augusta* as well and the vision of the Romans as civilizers *in hoc tam barbaro mundo*. So too the white Afrikaner Boer and his ethics, that potent brew of Seneca and Calvin, beating back the barbarian not at the gates, but in his own backyard. Notably, one of the letterheads considered by the executive committee of CASA a few months before this conference (November 1958) was the tomb of Mausolus at Halicarnassus, 'symbolizing the appreciation of the Classical heritage in a non-Classical world'.[44] Haarhoff seems to have shared this sentiment, as his paternalistic comments about 'the Bantu', trapped in eternal childhood, reliant on the nurturing love of virtuous Boer and sophisticated Brit, reveal (Whitaker 1997: 10).

Trans oceanum: from overseas

In his *oratio*, Haarhoff also expresses his joy that in the collection presented to him there are represented such famous classicists *trans oceanum* (from overseas). A constant concern among South African classicists during the *apartheid* era (a legacy which persists) was the inferiority complex of the colonial academic measured against the scholarly *gravitas* of the colonizer 'from overseas'. This combined with Afrikaner nationalism to spawn an intellectual xenophobia fraught with ambiguity, which feared the foreigner and courted *him* (used deliberately) at the same time.

One foreign nation, outside perfidious Albion's sphere of influence, was not yet feared and that was the Netherlands. As a result of the post-graduate training which many of the founding members had received in the Netherlands (where Dr Verwoerd, incidentally, was born), links with Dutch scholars in the early years were scrupulously maintained. At CASA's second conference a Dutch scholar delivered a paper and arrangements were made with the Netherlands-South Africa Cultural Exchange for the visit of Professor Wagenvoort from Utrecht (1957), conveniently also a deacon in the Dutch Reformed Church. Although Wagenvoort visited English-speaking universities during his visit (Henderson 2004: 94), it is obvious that the association in its earlier years preferred Dutch to English-speaking visitors who could neither understand nor promote the cause of Afrikaans.[45] In addition, as South Africa had by this stage violated the Universal Declaration of Human

Rights (1948) frequently and with impunity, English-speaking scholars from the UK and USA, not protected by the Netherlands-South Africa cultural accord (Genootskap Nederland-Suid-Afrika), could have tarnished CASA with the international opprobrium which the country as a whole was beginning to attract, largely because of the litany of legislation passed in 1949-1950: the Prohibition of Mixed Marriages Act (1949), the Population Registration Act (1950), the Group Areas Act (1950), the Immorality Amendment Act (1950) (Davenport 1991: 328).[46]

Ever alert to its international academic reputation, the Association had sent Gonin (its first chairman) to Avignon in 1956 to the first meeting of FIEC, the International Federation of the Societies of Classical Studies (Henderson 2004: 90), affiliation to which was still being investigated four years later (ibid.: 104); as president of FIEC, van Groningen of the University of Leiden had written to Viljoen, one of CASA's founding members and later Minister of Education in the Nationalist government, encouraging South Africa to become a member of the international organization.[47] For his efforts he was rewarded with an invitation to visit the country in 1960; one of the reasons proffered for the invitation was his 'kindly disposition to South Africa' (Henderson 2004: 107) which, in the political parlance of the times, meant at the very least that he did not openly disapprove of South Africa's political policies. Verwoerd, it must be remembered, had been elected Prime Minister in 1958 with an increased (white) majority (for the National Party) and in 1960 South Africa was on the brink of becoming a republic and leaving the Commonwealth.

CASA and the protection of Latin in schools

In 1918 when the University of the Cape of Good Hope became the University of South Africa, Latin was abolished as a compulsory subject for entrance to a university (ibid.: 29), which meant that the position of Latin in both schools and universities was threatened. The precarious relationship between the study of Classics and political power and the perceived need for a Classical Association to ingratiate itself with those who controlled the curriculum in state schools has long been a feature of the study of Classics in South Africa.[48]

In the years before the declaration of the Republic and afterwards, the Classical Association did not confine itself to the universities, but forged strong links with white schools, where Latin was taught, through the regional branches of the association that were gradually established between 1956 and 1967 in each of the four provinces.[49] Latin, as a third language, was still a subject offered for matriculation from high school (and hence university entrance) and it was in the interests of the Association to ensure that Latin maintained its privileged position in the high schools, thus ensuring (it was hoped) a steady stream of Classics students into the universities, where post-matriculation Latin was a compulsory subject for a degree in law (and Roman-Dutch law at that). Whenever the position of Latin in the schools and the universities became threatened in any way, for instance, by the introduction of an African language as a third language for matriculation and hence in direct competition with Latin, or a proposed bill to abolish Latin for attorneys, the Association leapt to the defence of Latin. In this way, it positioned itself as conservatively Euro-centric and elitist, opposed to African culture, rather than alongside it, even as the policy of separate development argued.[50] CASA even tried (in 1961) to get Latin retained in the seminaries of Afrikaans and English Protestant churches, but failed (Henderson 2005: 110, 112).

Sessions at some of the early conferences were devoted to problems in the high school Latin curriculum – for instance, how much Roman history or classical culture should be taught, the correct pronunciation of Latin, and how literary texts could be interpreted (Henderson 2004: 98, 99, 107). The high school syllabus, centred almost exclusively on Caesar and Cicero, Vergil and Ovid (not the naughty bits!) was carefully policed by CASA which commemorated, for instance, the death of Caesar and Cicero and the birth of Ovid in 1959 with coverage in the press and on the radio.[51] This close attention to publicity for the Classics, a constant feature of the various branch activities of CASA during the 1960s and 1970s, must be read against the progressive decline in the numbers of matriculants taking Latin, particularly when expressed as a percentage of the ever-increasing total number of candidates.[52] Thus long before the abolition of the Latin requirement for lawyers and the protected position of Latin as one of the third languages for matricula-tion, the warning signs were flashing and the records of CASA reflect the regular elegiac laments for its passing.[53] The State President of South Africa expresses his concern about the decline in interest in the Classics in 1966 (Henderson 2006: 136); CASA proposes a deputation to the Director of Education in 1973 in order to discuss the threatened position of Latin in the new differentiated school curriculum. To no avail.

What these statistics and laments reveal is that Latin, despite the close relationship between CASA and the organs of power, was in danger right from the very foundation of CASA and that, had CASA been steered by scholars less seduced by Afrikaner nationalism and invested in its dominance, steps would have been taken to promote Latin (and the Classics) in black schools in order, if anything, to ensure the future survival of the discipline. At that stage, however, in South Africa's fraught history, it must have seemed, even to the highly intelligent men on the CASA executive, that white rule on the southern tip of South Africa was destined to last for generations and Latin would still serve as a marker of an educated and ruling élite, and as the gateway to certain professions (the law and medicine especially).

CASA and the Extension of University Education Act (1959)

In the same year as CASA's third conference in Bloemfontein (1959), at which Haarhoff was presented with the first edition of *Acta Classica* (see above), the government passed its inappropriately-named Extension of University Education Act which, in keeping with *apartheid* ideology, established separate university colleges for the different 'ethnic groups'. Blacks, except under very specific conditions and with ministerial approval, could no longer attend 'White' state-aided universities and had to enrol at one of the designated state-controlled colleges – the University College of the North at Turfloop (for Sothos), the University College of Zululand at Ngoya (for Zulus), the University College for Indians, Durban, and the University College of the Western Cape, Bellville (for Coloureds). The University College of Fort Hare, already in existence, was transferred to the Ministry of Bantu Education and was designated for Xhosas.[54]

Because these colleges, before they became independent universities with their own examining bodies, had to write examinations set by the University of South Africa (UNISA), where there was a strong Classics Department, and because Latin was still required for the study of law and New Testament Greek for the study of theology and the training of

52

ministers, departments of Classics (or in some cases, separate departments of Latin and Greek) had to be established at these universities, in keeping with the 'separate but equal' ideology of *apartheid*. Although CASA's records indicate that classicists from these universities attended conferences and regional meetings (Henderson 2006: 146-7, 154-5), there is no record whatsoever of any acknowledgement by the CASA executive that now there would be more black students than ever before studying Latin, Greek and Classical Civilization and, as such, special attention should be paid to the promotion of the Classics at these universities, if the future of Classics in South Africa was to be assured. This is not surprising. Classicists at these universities were, on the whole, Afrikaans-speaking white males, and because these institutions were state-controlled, it is unlikely that any classicist who openly opposed the government's policies would have been appointed in the first place. Consequently, most members of CASA would have considered the educational enterprise at these 'tribal colleges' with Haarhoffian paternalism and a sense of the absolute rectitude of the separatist path on which the organization was already set. This separatism is evident, for instance, in the theme of 'Africa' chosen by one of the regional branches in 1963. Only *North* Africa and Hellenism, Christianity, and Roman imperial policy towards minority groups like the Jews are considered (Henderson 2005: 118). The possibilities of *South* Africa, its peoples and the relevance of the Classics to their cultures are ignored.

CASA's separatism also raises the question of the historiography of the organization. With the exception of Smuts' perceptive articles, this has been archival and somewhat hagiographical,[55] exclusively focused on Classics for whites, as determined by the Association's primary source material. When CASA was established in 1956, there seemed to be no awareness at all that blacks had been or were studying the Classics (and Latin in particular) at institutions like Lovedale and Zonnebloem in the Cape, at the South African Native College (later the University of Fort Hare), where D.D.T. Jabavu had been teaching Latin since 1916 (see Chapter 3), at many mission schools (especially those run by the Roman Catholic Church), at some 'Indian' and 'Coloured' schools, at seminaries and at the 'open' universities (before 1959). Of this tradition, CASA's records are completely silent, as silent as they are about the classical tradition in Anglophone, Francophone and Lusophone Africa.[56]

Totsiens to the Commonwealth: the price of
identity politics

When thirty members of CASA gathered for the fourth conference at Grahamstown in February 1961, South African society was irrevocably altered. Harold Macmillan, the British Prime Minister, had given his 'wind of change' speech to parliamentarians in Cape Town early in 1960, the wind being the chill blasts of decolonization throughout Africa. The Sharpeville massacre had occurred on 21 March 1960. International condemnation ensued. The black political movements, the Pan African Congress (PAC) and the African National Congress (ANC), had been banned. A state of emergency (the first of many) had been declared. Many activists were banned and/or detained without trial. Shortly after Sharpeville, the first (unsuccessful) assassination attempt on Verwoerd was perpetrated (Hepple 1967: 154). South Africa's white voters had, with the exception of predominantly English-speaking voters in Natal, voted for a republic (Davenport 1991: 354-61). In March 1961 South Africa left the Commonwealth and on 31 May 1961 South Africa became a republic. In the same year, Nelson Mandela, who had been acquitted after the lengthy treason trials (1956-1961), became the leader of the armed wing of the ANC. Many academics left South Africa in this year, including the English-speaking Vice-Chairman of CASA, K.D. White (Henderson 2005: 111 n.14).

Predictably, there is no awareness of the wider South African context in any of the papers given or deliberations made at the conference. It could be argued that one could and should expect nothing else at a Classics conference in South Africa in 1961 (or anywhere else for that matter). By its very nature, the study of Classics, especially in the early sixties before 1968 and the conscious politicization of knowledge, seemed remote from political and social realities. However, the fact that a small group of mainly Afrikaans-speaking white men – one woman gave a paper at the conference[57] – met for an academic conference in South Africa in 1961, at which the presidential address was on 'The Roman Concept of Natural Law', and issued an invitation to the Chief Justice of South Africa to be patron of the organization and to the High Commissioner in London (later the Minister of Foreign Affairs) to be an Honorary Vice-President (*Acta Classica* 4, 1961: 123) seems to me to be a profoundly political act, positioning the Classical Association within the ruling power élite and allied to two political appointees. There could be no doubt where the sympathies of the majority of CASA members lay. Confronted by the insularity of the Classical Association during these tumultuous years, one cannot but recall Verwoerd's words (1957): 'the plight of my people cannot be remedied except by political machinery' (Hepple 1967: 35). The political machinery was by now so well oiled that its dark satanic mills included academic and cultural associations, even if they seemed blissfully and suicidally unaware of it. For, under the law of the land, academic associations, such as the Classical Association, were for whites only.

In the years after the establishment of the Republic, the Classical Association continued with its biennial conferences and with the annual publication of its journal *Acta Classica*. Significantly, under the guidance of the founding fathers and their obvious commitment to Afrikaner nationalism, the highest percentage of articles written in Afrikaans occurs in the decade 1958-1967, when Viljoen and Gonin were managing editors of the journal;[58] the percentage of reviews in Afrikaans is predictably higher, because of the journal's policy to publish reviews of works written by South African classicists (or classicists working in South Africa) and because translations of Greek and Roman authors into Afrikaans have always been foregrounded by the journal.[59] Another notable fact is that the number of 'appreciations/*waarderinge*' and obituaries published to honour Afrikaans-speaking scholars or scholars at traditionally Afrikaans-speaking universities greatly outnumbers those of English-speaking classicists throughout the journal's history.[60] Of the founding fathers, Smuts, de Kock, Gonin, van Rooy and Naudé receive obituaries in *Acta Classica*; three of these (Smuts, de Kock, Gonin) are written in Afrikaans.[61] Smuts, de Kock and Naudé also receive obituaries in *Akroterion*, now the second journal of the Classical Association, all written in Afrikaans.[62] Obituaries for English-speaking classicists, including professors, seem to be banished to the pages of *Akroterion* where they outnumber those for Afrikaans-speaking scholars.[63] As there is clearly no distinct 'obituary policy' laid down in the constitution of the organization, what does emerge, whether deliberate or not, is that the careers and contributions of Afrikaans-speaking scholars to the study and teaching of the Classics in South Africa have been honoured and promoted by the editors of CASA's official journals at the expense of English-speaking scholars at traditionally English-speaking universities.[64] One could argue that the readership of *Akroterion* during the 1970s and 1980s was more extensive than that of *Acta Classica*, which seemed destined for a lonely spinsterhood on the shelves of university libraries, and latterly in cyberspace, but the international exposure provided by *Acta Classica* was obviously greater, as is evident from the list of many foreign journals received in exchange.

Of the preoccupations of the Association, established in the foundation years, little changes in the subsequent decades, as one peruses the pages of *Akroterion* and reads the *Varia Didactica* and reports of the various branches, apart from the defence of Latin in the (white) schools and universities, which grows more strident over the years.

At CASA's first colloquium in 1982, devoted to elementary Latin and Greek courses at university level, Professor Kriel, then chairman of the association, warns of the demise of Latin in the schools: 'unless a drastic change occurs in our South African school system, the day can be foreseen when Latin will no longer be taught at school, and all students will make their first acquaintance with Latin in an introductory course at university' (1982: 87). Again, Kriel, commenting on the de Lange report (a Human Sciences Research Council's investigation into education in South Africa) and its over-emphasis on the need for practical skills and the requirements of the job market, laments the report's 'disastrous implications' for the teaching of the Classics and any other 'cultural subjects' in South African schools (1983: 5). As far as a 'genuine Latin 1 course as prerequisite for legal qualification is concerned', Kriel considers that recent judgments imply that 'the writing is on the wall' for this requirement (ibid.: 7).[65] Styling himself as a 'Jeremiah of old', Kriel, convinced that the study of Classics has something relevant to say to every 'population group' in South Africa, makes this impassioned plea; 'we have no time to waste in deciding whether we have something to say, something vitally important to offer to *all* of us in southern Africa' (ibid.: 9). It is noteworthy how progressively inclusive the discourse about the value of Classics in South Africa becomes as the country moves inexorably towards the first democratic elections and black majority rule.

In the very year of the first democratic elections (1994), a real sense of crisis is evident in the Association's records when the Latin requirement for the *Admission of Advocates Act* (no. 74 of 1964) is scrapped in December of that year. Almost overnight departments of Classics at

South African universities experienced sharp falls in enrolments especially in the large Introductory Latin classes which had kept many departments afloat. Staff were deployed elsewhere or retrenched, and some departments eventually closed altogether.[66] Writing from the University of Stellenbosch, Jo-Marie Claassen, who had worked especially hard to promote Latin in the schools by means of a biennial Latin Olympiad, greets the news with a sense of optimism and liberation from a tiresome prescription which had hampered, rather than promoted, the cause of Latin and the Classics. 'The challenge is ours', she writes, 'to offer a Classics curriculum that is vibrant, relevant, exciting and educating. The position of Latin at school and at university is still as strong as the enthusiasm of its proponents can make it' (1995: 62). Like Kriel, she adopts the discourse of inclusivity and, in the course of celebrating South African's eleven official languages and its multi-lingual diversity, encourages Latin teachers to familiarize themselves with the nine official African languages (where appropriate) in order to teach Latin more effectively in a multi-cultural classroom. She even draws attention to the classical tradition amongst Xhosa-speaking South Africans at Lovedale (now the University of Fort Hare) in the nineteenth century – a tradition ignored by the founding *patres* of CASA (see Chapter 3).

The voices of Kriel and Claassen, Afrikaans-speaking scholars at the Universities of Pretoria and Stellenbosch respectively, reveal that the exploration of Afrikaner identity on the cultural and intellectual terrain was no longer deemed necessary in the 1980s and 1990s and that the politics of the period and the decline of Latin in the schools and the universities shaped a keen awareness of a multi-cultural identity, which would have been entirely alien to classical scholars in the 1950s and 1960s.[67] Haarhoff's paternalistic position in relation to African cultures surfaces momentarily in Kriel's work, when he argues that the South African classicist has an urgent task 'to hand over to others the treasures (as opposed to the trash) of Western culture, so that these treasures can impregnate and fertilize indigenous cultures', with a reference to Dr Banda's 'prestigious' school in Malawi, now an eccentric instance of post-colonial absurdity (1983: 9). Claassen celebrates the end of colonialism (1995: 61); Kriel reveals that he has internalized many of its prejudices, despite embracing a wider inclusivity than that for which Haarhoff was well known.

In April 2009 Gerrit van Niekerk Viljoen, one of the most energetic of the founding *patres* and certainly the most politically involved South African classicist since Hofmeyr, died (see Chapter 2).[68] Chief editor of *Acta Classica* from 1959 until 1966, he resigned his professorial post at the University of South Africa to become Rector of the Rand Afrikaans University in 1967. At the invitation of P.W. Botha, who was Prime Minister at the time, he was appointed Administrator-General of what was then South West Africa (now Namibia) in 1978 and subsequently served as Minister of Education (later Minister of Co-operation, Development and Education) from 1984 until 1989 – during this period he made it clear that he was opposed to racial integration in state schools (Davenport 1991: 423). Subsequently Minister of Constitutional Development from 1989 until 1992, he retired from public life, exhausted by the stress of participating in CODESA (the Convention for a Democratic South Africa). Educated at the Universities of Pretoria, Cambridge and Leiden, where he completed a doctorate on Pindar, Viljoen was also a founder member of the Union of Afrikaans Students (1948) and chairman of the Afrikaner Broederbond from 1974 until 1980. As Giliomee and Mbenga rightly emphasize, the Broederbond, founded in 1918, 'exercised its greatest influence in the spheres of education and culture' (2008: 289), particularly through the Federasie van Afrikaanse Kultuurvereniginge ('the Federation of Afrikaans Cultural Associations'), which eventually controlled almost all Afrikaner cultural associations. Because the Broederbond became a secret organization in 1929, it is not absolutely clear how many of the other founding *patres* were members of the Bond, although selective membership lists have been published (e.g. Serfontein 1979): what is clear is that the careers of a number of prominent South African classicists at Afrikaans-speaking universities suffered because they were *not* members of the Bond, one directly because of Viljoen's intervention.

Viljoen's involvement in CASA, in national politics as a member of the ruling National Party, and in Afrikaner identity politics, especially as chairman of the Broederbond, is the clearest expression of how deeply the Classical Association in its formative years was implicated in Afrikaner nationalist ideology. Features of his career, such as his post-graduate education in the Netherlands and his profound commitment to Afrikaner causes, whilst a student at the University of Pretoria and when Rector of the Rand Afrikaans University, are common to most of the influential founding fathers. Other aspects of his career – his education at Cambridge and his administrative excellence – provide interesting links with previous South African classicists involved in politics and with many British colonial administrators whose study of the Classics seemed to have prepared them for imperial rule (see Chapter 2). His death marks the final passing of the foundation era, but not necessarily the liberation of the study of Classics in South Africa from the 'mind forg'd manacles' of Afrikaner nationalist ideology.

The Classics and English-speaking South African Identities

If Oxford would ... turn from the Greeks to the Negroes it would help as nothing else would.

Jan Smuts, quoted in Maylam 2005: 76

An imperial library in the Cape Colony

For that arch-imperialist, Cecil John Rhodes, whose last will and testament included a quotation from one of Horace's *Odes*,[1] two works constituted his favourite reading: Marcus Aurelius' *Meditations*, which he underlined assiduously and carried around with him, and Gibbon's *Decline and Fall of the Roman Empire*.[2] So interested was he in Gibbon's work that, on a visit to England in 1893, he arranged to have all the original Greek and Latin sources used by Gibbon translated into English, as his own Greek and Latin were 'deficient' (Rotberg 1988: 386).

Arthur Humphreys of Hatchards, London's famous bookshop, assembled a group of thirty scholars together and these 'men, matrons and maids', some of whom were ex-dons of Oxbridge colleges who had 'drifted into matrimony', slaved away in the British Museum Reading Room translating Gibbon's sources (ibid.: 386). The translators were sworn to secrecy, in keeping with Rhodes's wishes, and their names never appeared on the works they translated. Gradually, over two hundred volumes of translations, bound in red Morocco with their titles engraved on the spines in gilt, were sent out to the Cape, before the project was cancelled in 1898, perhaps because of the exorbitant cost (Wardle 1993: 87). These volumes, or those which were not destroyed in the fire of 1896, are housed in the library at Groote Schuur, the mansion in Cape Dutch style which Rhodes leased in 1891, bought in 1893 and bequeathed to South Africa on his death in 1902 (Rotberg 1988: 380,

666). Since 1911, Prime Ministers and, more recently, Vice-Presidents of South Africa have made Groote Schuur their home.

For many years during the *apartheid* era, classicists at the University of Cape Town attempted, without success, to gain access to the library in order to evaluate and arrange publication of the translations of the rarer authors whose works have not been published since the project was undertaken (Wardle 1993: 88). Permission was finally granted in 1992 and, in the opinion of Wardle, who made a 'brief perusal' of a selection of the volumes, the anonymous translations, some of which include the corrections of proof-readers, are of a high standard (ibid.).

What is significant about the establishment of the library and, of course the purchase of the estate and its refurbishment, was that it occurred during Rhodes's premiership of the Cape Colony (1890-1896), when he guilefully exploited Cape politics, his friendship with Hofmeyr, and his alliance with the Afrikaner Bond in order to further his imperialist designs in the territories north of the Limpopo.[3] To woo the Afrikaner Bond, which was potentially the most powerful group in the Cape Parliament, he gave his support (and often his money) to those very causes which he knew were most dear to the hearts of Cape Afrikaners: in 1882 he supported Hofmeyr's bill permitting the use of Dutch as a parliamentary language, he reneged on his capitalist principles and opposed heavy taxes on wine and brandy, thus wedding himself to the protectionist principles of Cape wine farmers and their parliamentary representatives, and he opposed the liberal non-racial franchise and made it clear that, as far as the 'native' policy, was concerned, he was on the side of the Afrikaner *Boer* (Giliomee and Mbenga 2008: 197). Strategies such as these cemented his relationship with Hofmeyr and the Bond and resulted in his election to the premiership in 1890.[4] During his premiership, further overtures were made to the Cape Afrikaners to solidify this dangerous alliance between British imperialism at its most Machiavellian and a vulnerable Afrikaner grouping sensitive to English arrogance and perfidy, especially in the wake of the discovery of gold in the Transvaal Republic in 1886 and its implications for the Cape economy, Rhodes's schemes to ensure control of the diamond-mining industry (1889), and economic problems suffered by Afrikaner wine and stock farmers during the late nineteenth century.[5]

When Rhodes leased the estate of Groote Schuur in 1891 and bought it two years later, there is no doubt that his retention of the Dutch name and his restoration, in Cape Dutch style, of a seventeenth century Dutch estate which had fallen into ruin were simply part of his strategy to win over the Afrikaner power bloc.[6] That he should furnish his library, where many of his subsequent imperialist schemes were hatched, including presumably the ill-conceived Jameson Raid (1895) which resulted in the rupture of the alliance with the Afrikaner Bond, the end of his warm friendship with Hofmeyr and the loss of Afrikaner trust in him, with translations of the Greek and Latin classics reflected his interest in the classical world nurtured both at school and at Oriel College, Oxford.[7] Furthermore the combination of British imperialist designs and a classical education, especially at Oxford, the intellectual home of the British colonial enterprise in the late nineteenth century, characterised the lives and careers of many governors, entrepreneurs, soldiers and administrators throughout the British empire.[8] As Rhodes himself described Oxford, it was 'a good mill for turning out Englishmen of a stamp fitted to either govern or develop the still unknown and measureless possibilities of Africa' (in Rotberg 1988: 106-7). Most ardent colonialists in Africa and elsewhere would have agreed with Rhodes, but few would have regarded a well-thumbed version of Marcus Aurelius as his 'most precious possession' (Rotberg 1988: 385). Rhodes is thus an unusual example of the convergence of the study of the Classics, the Imperial Project and education at an élite university like Oxford.

Rotberg has analysed the 101 passages underlined by Rhodes in the edition of Marcus Aurelius' *Meditations* he so admired (translated by George Long, 1880) that he referred to it as his 'guide in life'. According to Rotberg, these reveal a 'preoccupation with four ideas': the inevitability of death as a necessary part of life, the obligatory dominance of reason over the emotions and passions, the need for hard work and exertion rather than pleasure and popularity, and, finally, the need for co-operation with others and flexibility of opinion, rather than inflexible self-reliance (1988: 384-5). With the possible exception of the first idea, Rhodes clearly struggled with the other three; hence, perhaps, the necessity to carry around the *Meditations* and underline precepts important to him.

Although the *Meditations* are an interesting blend of Stoicism, Epicureanism and Platonism, Rhodes's underlined ideas constitute the very essence of Stoicism, which Marcus Aurelius admired in Epictetus, one of Rhodes's favourites too. Rhodes seems to have been especially attracted to the Roman emperors: he believed that in looks he resembled Titus, but in thought Hadrian, who was Marcus Aurelius' uncle and loving benefactor. Because of this interest, and Victorian scholarly interest generally in comparisons between the Roman and British empires,[9] Hatchard had included amongst the books shipped out to the Cape eighteen biographies of Roman emperors (Rotberg 1988: 386-7). As Vasunia, following Majeed, has shown, 'the very method of comparative enquiry was deeply and inextricably entangled in British imperialist practices and discourses' (2005: 59).

This presumably accounts for Rhodes's great interest in Gibbon's work, but Rotberg does refer to the 'glories of Rome as well as its [Gibbon's *Decline and Fall*] celebration of the virtues of celibacy for pre-medieval popes' which 'inspired his vision of his own and Britain's imperial destiny' (1988: 386). Rotberg, in collaboration with Miles Shore, offers some imaginative psycho-analytical insights into Rhodes's celibacy and his Hadrianic homosexuality, crystallised perhaps by the homosociality of college life in Oxford at the same time as Oscar Wilde.[10] Notable is the collection of translations of Erotic Epigrams, not used by Gibbon, in his library which includes Greek pederastic poetry 'completely unabridged', as Rhodes had instructed should be the guiding principle for all translations (Wardle 1993: 86).

An Afrikaans administrator, Rhodes Scholar and Oxford-educated classicist

When Rhodes was Premier of the Cape Colony (1894), Jan Hendrik Hofmeyr, whose father's cousin was the Hofmeyr ('Onze Jan'), who was a close political ally and friend of Rhodes until 1896, was born in Cape Town.[11] Educated at the South African College where he obtained his BA (Honours) at the age of fifteen and MA in Classics at seventeen, he benefited from the Rhodes Scholarships established by Rhodes's will and went to Balliol College, Oxford, where he read Classics, achieving first-class passes in both Mods and Greats (1913-1916): he was later made an Honorary Fellow of Balliol (the first South African to receive such an honour) and received an honorary doctorate from Oxford.

On his return to South Africa in 1916, he was appointed as a lecturer in Latin at his former college (soon to be the University of Cape Town); a year later he had moved to the University College of the Witwatersrand (then known as the School of Mines), where he was appointed Professor of Classics at the age of twenty two. His appointment to the chair of Greek at his *alma mater* was pre-empted by his astonishing elevation, at the age of twenty three, to the principalship of the University College of the Witwatersrand in 1919. During his tenure of office, he began to refine the prodigious administrative skills which characterised his subsequent career and to learn something, in his tense relationship with the university's Senate, of the meaning of academic freedom.[12] Despite his heavy workload, he managed to publish, with Haarhoff (whom we have already met in Chapter 1), 'Studies in Ancient Imperialism' (1921),[13] before leaving academic life to become Administrator of the Transvaal in 1924, at the invitation of General Smuts. Elected as Vice Chancellor of the University in 1926, and eventually Chancellor in 1938, he entered political life in 1929 and became a Member of Parliament as a supporter of Smuts's South African Party, before it formed a coalition with Hertzog's National Party to become the United Party in 1934.[14] In Hertzog's government, Hofmeyr took on the portfolios of Education, Interior and Public Health (simultaneously).

When the party split over whether South Africa should enter the Second World War on Britain's side, Hofmeyr, arguing that the neutrality proposed by Hertzog would result in South Africa's departure from the British Empire,[15] remained in the Smuts government to serve as Minister of Finance and Education (1939-1948) and, in Smuts's frequent wartime absences, as Acting Prime Minister. He died in 1948, the very year when the United Party lost the general election to the Nationalist Party, a loss blamed by many political commentators of the period, including Smuts's son, on Hofmeyr's liberal racial views (Paton 1964: 490-505).

Hofmeyr's views on race and integration were certainly liberal, in contrast to the rigid separatism and inflammatory racism Malan and his Nationalist followers used to win the post-war election, but he never clarified what he really meant by his famous remark made in Parliament in 1946 that he was in favour of the 'ultimate removal of the colour bar from the Constitution' in the 'political sphere' (ibid.: 446). The party to which he belonged certainly did not uphold these views. In fact, even though he was a member of the ruling party and the cabinet, he opposed the infamous Hertzog Bills (1936) which disenfranchised black voters in the Cape,[16] protested vigorously against Hertzog's appointment of an unqualified Afrikaner as the ministerial representative of the Coloureds in Parliament (1938) and was often vilified by the Afrikaner press for his non-racial views, which included support for the rights of Indians and Jews in South Africa. In 1948, he dismissed *apartheid* as conceived by the Nationalists, as a 'cloak for repression and nothing else' (Higgs 1997: 147).

Hofmeyr's most distinguished biographer, Alan Paton, frequently comments on Hofmeyr's 'enigmatic' or ambivalent identity, evident, for instance, in his love for Oxford, the English language and culture, and his dislike of the arrogance of the English public school boy he met there: 'it was the dislike of the 'colonial' for a self-assurance that made him feel uncouth ...' (1964: 32). A champion of the Afrikaans language, his home tongue, Hofmeyr was nonetheless opposed to an exclusive Afrikaner nationalism. Paton captures this ambivalence well:

As for his culture, it was certainly not Afrikaans, but it was equally certain not English; it was the culture of a man of the world (though not in a worldly sense), of a Christian and humanist, versed in the classics, and an admirer of British institutions. He was, however, no cosmopolitan – he was much more a South African. But narrow allegiances, especially when they were exclusive and intolerant, were distasteful to him (ibid.: 68).

This attitude is reflected in his politics as well: he supported the idea of a republican South Africa within the British Empire, but dismissed as 'Republican nonsense' a completely independent South Africa freed from what was perceived by Afrikaner nationalists as the yoke of British imperialism (ibid.: 86-7). For attitudes such as these, and for his support of South Africa's declaration of war on Germany, his Afrikaner critics denounced him as 'un-South African' (ibid.: 329). The Nationalist Strijdom regarded him as one of the

greatest threats to Afrikanerdom, because of his lack of devotion to Afrikaner things, his 'English' mind, his espousal of dangerous ideals of racial equality that if realised would destroy white civilization in Africa (ibid.: 351).

On Pan-African political platforms, for instance in response to the suggestion (in 1936) that Germany should regain its colonial presence in Africa, Hofmeyr referred to himself, in an interview in Dar-es-Salaam, as an African:

> If Africans are to be treated as pawns in the European game, then it is right for us as fellow-Africans to stand together and say, 'Hands off Africa' (quoted in Paton 1964: 247).

As Rhodes exemplifies the imperialist British entrepreneur who read Classics at Oxford, so Hofmeyr embodies the tradition of the enlightened Cape Afrikaner. Similarly, Haarhoff, who was also educated at the South African College and Oxford (Worcester College), where he too was a Rhodes Scholar, before succeeding Hofmeyr in the chair of Classics at the University of the Witwatersrand. Both benefited from British colonialism, yet at the same time were passionately loyal to Afrikaans and Afrikaner nationality, itself in many ways the production of the very system which provided the classical education of the best representatives of their class. Tamarkin (1996) has skilfully shown how the ambiguities of British colonialism and Cape Afrikaner identity unravelled on the political stage, particularly in the relationship between Rhodes and Hofmeyr ('Onze Jan'), the relation of the classicist turned politician. The careers of the classicists, Hofmeyr and Haarhoff, illustrate how the ambiguities of this identity unravel on the intellectual and cultural terrain. Both profit from their allegiance to the centres of power, yet both suffer, precisely because they contest one of the building blocks of Afrikaner ideology: racial and racist separatism.[17] Hofmeyr's opposition to this, and to a lesser extent Haarhoff's, may well hark back to the influence of the liberal Gilbert Murray, whom both encountered at Oxford and to whom Haarhoff dedicated his *Vergil and South Africa* with the flattering 'Gilberto Murray Humanitatis Exemplari Insignissimo' (For Gilbert Murray, a most distinguished example of humaneness).

The Oxford connection in Natal

As the study of the Classics at Oxford certainly contributed to the formation of the interesting and complex identities of Afrikaners like Hofmeyr and Haarhoff, so Oxford-educated classicists played an important role in the development of the identities of many English-speaking white South African students of the Classics at what were regarded, during the *apartheid* era, as the English-speaking universities (Cape Town, Natal, Witwatersrand and Rhodes), generally opposed to Nationalist Party rule and enforced segregation.

As an example of such a university, I am going to concentrate on the Department of Classics at the then University of Natal (Pietermaritzburg) in the 1970s and 1980s, when the Oxford connection was particularly strong and opposition on the campus to the atrocities of the Nationalist regime especially vociferous. To assess the influence of Oxonians on the study of the Classics and identity formation, I shall focus on public discourses, in particular on the inaugural lectures of three successive Professors of Classics at the University of Natal: David Raven (16 May 1973), Magnus Henderson (24 May 1978) and Geoffrey Chapman (15 August 1984).

Formerly Dean of Trinity College, Oxford, and author of works such as *Latin Metre: an Introduction* (1965) and its companion on *Greek Metre* (1968), Raven came out to Natal in 1971 and was appointed to the Chair of Classics in 1973 in the department established by the Cambridge-educated Petrie (see Chapter 1), who was present at the lecture (then aged ninety two).

From the Latin elegiacs on the cover of the published version of the lecture addressed to Whiteley, another Oxford graduate in the Classics Department on the Durban campus of the university who had sent his good wishes for the occasion, to the opening words in Latin, Raven's inaugural lecture entitled 'The Role of Classical Studies in the 1970s' opens as one would expect from an Oxonian inaugural lecture in the colonies – self-consciously clever and aimed at both impressing and intimidating the audience, consisting of (white) fellow academics and (white) members of the general public. However, after the rhetorical opening, the speech becomes an interesting blend of self-irony, critique of traditional British classical education and its association with Empire, the inevitable condescension, and pragmatic advice.

Raven eschews answering the question '*why* study the Classics at all in the 1970s?', but then cannot resist offering what he regards as 'a hackneyed answer in hackneyed terms' (1973: 2). Hackneyed it certainly is, but not unfamiliar in contemporary South Africa – in order to

68

appreciate properly 'the evolution of modern Western society' and 'the growth of our own language', we need to study the ancient Greek and Roman tradition which 'underlies an astonishing proportion of what we ourselves have inherited and developed' (ibid.: 2). Raven then turns to answering, at some length, what he perceives as the more difficult question: '*how* to study the Classics in the 1970s?' Before a vigorous critique of the Victorian approach to the Classics, traces of which he finds in the teaching of Latin in some South African schools, Raven reflects on the teaching of Classics in British schools and universities with the following introduction:

> I shall be speaking, predominantly, about British schools and universities, not through an insular belief in their own superiority (indeed, from the point of view of Classical teaching, in many ways they have proved inferior to the German academies), but because it is from them, obviously, that our own Classical tradition in Natal is mainly derived; and I shall speak, at some stages, more about British schools than about British universities because it is to their academic level that Classical teaching at South African universities can most readily be related (1973: 3-4).

Beginning with an account of the tyranny of Classics at Dr Arnold's Rugby, Raven accuses the Victorian public-school and British university system of producing a 'curious heresy about the Classics which is still far from dead': that the Greeks and Romans were 'really rather like the Victorians, in all sorts of ways in which, to be frank, they surely were not' (ibid.: 4). Amusingly deconstructing the relationship between the three Cs – Classics, Christianity and Cricket – he dwells in some detail on a typical Victorian school curriculum and deplores the inordinate amount of time and effort spent on memorising Latin and Greek accidence and syntax, and on churning out verse and prose compositions in Greek and Latin, without reference to or appreciation of the literature and culture of the Greeks and Romans (ibid.: 6-10).

Turning to the twentieth century in which he sees at first 'a dignified withdrawal' rather than 'an adventurous regrouping' in reaction to the Victorian system, Raven gives an account of how the teaching of Classics in modern Britain has adapted (or not adapted) to the dethronement of Classics from its dominant place in the curriculum and to the consequent decline in the numbers of students studying Greek and Latin at both schools and universities.

After a catalogue of the advances in modern research in the Classics – in archaeology (Troy, Crete, Mycenaean sites in mainland Greece, Pompeii, Roman Britain), language (the decipherment of Linear B), literature (especially as regards Homer and oral epic) and in the appreciation of Classical architecture, sculpture and vase-painting – Raven concludes that 'our attitude to the Classics has been freshened' (ibid.: 13) and adds the following:

> I must not omit the influence, particularly in my own University of Oxford, of German scholarship on the British Classical approach: the Germanic mixture of austere analysis with literary sensitivity, which characterised such scholars as Maas and Fraenkel, finding asylum in England and gloriously stimulating British scholarship (ibid.: 13-14).

As an aspect of this fresh approach, Raven briefly discusses the advantages and disadvantages of the new approaches to Latin teaching – in particular the Nuffield Foundation's *Cambridge Latin Course* which he strongly recommends to the school teachers in the audience, although he questions the suitability of its use for beginners at university level, objecting to the puerility of some of the subject matter. Far more impressed is he by the McGill Greek project which he had himself used with beginners at Oxford.

In the last section of his inaugural, Raven turns to Classics in South Africa and in Natal. He praises the Department for its courses in Classical Civilization (the literature, history, philosophy, art and society of the ancient world in translation) which he hopes will develop into a major subject (as opposed to a one-year minor) and declares that the department will adopt modern approaches to the teaching of the languages, including the *Cambridge Latin Course* already in use for Introductory Latin, mainly for cohorts of aspirant lawyers. Raven briefly comments on his experience of South African students who have come up to university with matriculation Latin: some of these have been taught by the Gradgrind method (parrot-learning and memorizing set-work translations in a cultural vacuum), but others are from schools where 'moderate and sensible linguistic discipline has been combined with lively interest in the ancient world, and it is a joy to know that such teaching exists in South African schools' (ibid.: 18-19). He offers some critique of the new common Latin syllabus and expresses the hope that the Natal Education Department will eventually accept Classical Civilization as a teaching subject in schools. Finally, in his peroration, Raven summarises what the Classics Department under his aegis hopes to achieve:

> We hope to achieve – and to help our students to achieve – insight, depth and perspective when looking at this vital part of our Western heritage, and observing its influence upon us. We shall compare the Greek and Roman civilizations with ours. We shall discover the extent and nature of various debts – the debt of Milton to Homer and Virgil, of modern drama to the Greek, of modern schools of philosophical thought to Plato. We may find possible historical lessons: some may find a lesson in the decline of Athens when (they may feel) too much leisure and too many impractical pursuits caused a city to become decadent and unmotivated; others may be interested by the inward-looking pointlessness of Sparta, where the need to keep down a subject population stifled the intellectual and cultural growth of a privileged citizen class. But on the whole we shall expect to find more differences than similarities: we shall try to avoid the Victorian heresy of 'updating' the thoughts and attitudes of ancient peoples (ibid.: 21).

The peroration continues in like manner with some Demosthenic flourishes until the final paragraph – a clarion call directed at the legion of university bureaucrats on the stage: 'The Classics are not *dead*: they live, and their survival in this utilitarian age is not an anachronism, but a proof of their abiding relevance and fascination' (ibid.: 22).

Raven's inaugural lecture is underpinned by attitudes and assumptions which seem to me to lie at the heart of the contribution of many Oxonians to the study of the Classics in South Africa and to the identity formation of many English-speaking South African classicists during this period. First, his use, throughout his lecture, of 'we' and 'our' ('our Western heritage', 'our language') includes the audience as part of the great British diaspora in the wake of Empire, as if British and South African English-speaking identities had merged, with a shared cultural and intellectual home, preferably in Oxford. No sensitivity is shown towards Afrikaans-speaking members of the audience, including the Professor of Afrikaans-Nederlands who was present, let alone the fact that the University of Natal is situated in a province with a vast majority of speakers of isiZulu.

Secondly, the apparent *humanitas* of this inclusiveness, for which Oxford's degree in Classics (*literae humaniores*) is well known, is coupled to a deliberate distancing of the audience from Oxford's standards. Students of the Classics in the audience are informed that their South African degrees 'can most readily be related' to standards in British schools, not universities: the South African matriculation in Latin is considered, without any empirical evidence, to be the standard of an English 'O level' (ibid.: 11). Good South African schools are patronised with faint praise: their 'moderate and sensible linguistic discipline' is extolled. A distinct hierarchy of classical excellence is established: at the top is German scholarship (this is not unexpected from one of Fraenkel's students), then British scholarship (or rather Oxford scholarship), then at the bottom of the heap, South African scholarship, earnestly trying to redeem itself from the stigma of being internationally third-rate. As a student of Raven, who was a passionate and inspiring teacher, I recall being constantly reminded that, at various stages of my degree, I was still x number of years behind an Oxford or Cambridge undergraduate of the same age. After four years of Latin and Greek at university – 'well, you are more or less at the standard of an average Mods student' and so on. 'If you ever get to Oxford, you will have to play catch-up' – as Rhodes had to.

This constant reminding of one's inferiority resulted, in my case and that of a number of other white English-speaking South African classicists, in the creation of an insecure academic identity, which intersected with the ambiguous identities of the Afrikaner classicists (see Chapter 1). Identity, like gender, is invariably relational, and in the complex scrum of South African identities jostling for coherence, a further hierarchy of classical competence was established. If English-speaking white South African classicists are inferior to their Oxonian counterparts, at least they are superior to Afrikaans-speaking classicists and the occasional black graduate produced by the 'tribal colleges'.[18] Although Raven never overtly expressed this perception in his inaugural, he certainly believed that this was 'true' of the 'South African context' and it was a perception repeatedly reinforced by Oxbridge-educated Classicists working in South Africa, especially at CASA conferences in the 1970s and 1980s.

In his inaugural, Raven takes great pains to demolish the Victorian approach to the teaching of the Classics, but in one respect he situates himself directly within late Victorian intellectual discourse: comparative studies. 'We shall compare the Greek and Roman civilization with ours': 'ours' referring not to South African or African cultures, but to a vague notion of a pan-Englishness, across the Channel no less, transcending boundaries of space and nationality. Raven warns against what he perceives as the dangers of the comparative approach as understood by the Victorians – the heresy of 'updating the thoughts and attitudes of ancient peoples' – and in the process makes a veiled political allusion to *apartheid* South Africa.

The words 'others may be interested by the inward-looking pointlessness of Sparta, where the need to keep down a subject population stifled the intellectual and cultural growth of a privileged citizen class' would have been interpreted by many in the audience as an allusion to the position of black, Indian and 'coloured' South Africans under Nationalist Party rule and to the complacent mediocrity of the privileged white middle classes which constituted by far the majority of students in the Classics in the 1970s (and still do). The allusion is veiled precisely because of the political atmosphere in which the lecture was delivered.[19]

Raven was a foreign national, and a year before (1972) a British member of the English department on the same campus had been deported because he had asked a class to stand for a minute's silence to commemorate the death of freedom of speech in South Africa. This 'subversive' activity had been reported to the Minister of Justice by one of the Security ('Special') Branch spies with which the campus was infested.[20] A year of simmering student unrest, of police swoops on the campus on which Raven lived (from the beginning of 1973) as the Warden of an all male residence, of persistent police brutality against protesting students (witnessed by the author) and the banning of student protests under the Riotous Assemblies Act (no. 17 of 1956), preceded the inaugural lecture and clearly informed its guarded political allusion.

On a national level, one event in particular had united staff and (most) students on the campus, especially those in the Humanities: South Africa's very own *Murder in the Cathedral*. On 2 June 1972, a police baton charge on two hundred students from the University of Cape Town, protesting against inequalities in Bantu Education outside St George's Cathedral in the city, had resulted in a wave of protests on the largely white English-speaking campuses. Some students had fled into the inner sanctum of the cathedral from where they were forcibly dragged by police and beaten.

In the students' newspaper of the Pietermaritzburg campus of the University of Natal (*NUX*), articles record the lively protests on the campus against police interference with the right to peaceful protest, the support of the local principal and staff, and the interpretations of various political commentators, from those perceiving the police brutalities as a revival of the 'Boer versus Brit' tension ('white-on-white' violence) to those cynically reminding readers that what the white protestors suffered was negligible compared to the daily sufferings of black South Africans.[21] In the first few months of 1973, which preceded Raven's inaugural, the biggest workers' strikes in South Africa for years, largely initiated by migrant Zulu workers, with roots in rural Natal, added to the political tensions on the campus, as a number of academics and students, in the intellectual aftermath of the student riots in Paris in 1968, had embraced Marxism and the trade union movement (Chipkin 2007: 85-7). Tensions between the Marxists, Liberals and right-wingers (frequently supporters of the United Party and/or Christian fundamentalists) were not unknown on the Pietermaritzburg campus and illustrate the fact that white, English-speaking South Africans, in opposition to *apartheid*, were not politically homogeneous. In an interview with *NUX* some months before his inaugural, Raven, in response to questions about reforms in the residence which he then headed, remarks:

As for the question of being conservative or liberal, I am a traditionalist, in the sense that to destroy the traditions of any community has even greater potential for harm than good. I was Dean of my Oxford college, a position very similar to this job. I was regarded as the sort of person who was so conservative as to be difficult to budge on some issues. (22 February 1973: 1)

2. The Classics and English-speaking South African Identities

Raven makes it abundantly clear, and this was true of many white English-speaking staff members and students, that one can protest against the cruelties of the *apartheid* state in the tradition of the liberal South African university, and yet be profoundly conservative. This seems to suggest a contradictory identity: the *uitlander* (like Raven) who was allied to powerful élites and had so obviously internalised the patronising voices of empire, yet generated, ever so tentatively, in the South African context, discourses which were resistant to power. In a subsequent public lecture, given as the first University Lecture of 1974 and provocatively entitled 'Why the Hell read the Classics?', Raven pointed out that one of the inducements to read the Classics in South Africa was that 'this literature was the only form of art to go uncensored in this country' (*NUX* 2, 14 March 1974: 2).

Rather as Sharpeville (1960) acted as a 'watershed' in South African politics, the Soweto riots, protesting against the compulsory use of Afrikaans in black schools, erupted in 1976, and many foreign academics left South Africa. Raven left the University of Natal for King's School, Canterbury, and William Watts, a charismatic and popular Latin teacher who had introduced the *Cambridge Latin Course* on the Pietermaritzburg campus, returned to his native Canada.

Magnus Henderson was Raven's successor in the Chair of Classics, and he delivered his inaugural lecture ('Alcibiades and the Ancient Historian') in 1978, seven months after the murder of the Black Consciousness leader, Steve Biko, in detention (12 September 1977). The edition of *NUX* which contained an article reporting Biko's death and giving the almost exclusively white readership some background to Black Consciousness was subsequently banned by the government (10 October 1978: 3).

Born in Zambia and educated at Rhodes University in Grahamstown, Henderson won a Rhodes Scholarship and read Classics at Balliol College, Oxford, where he was tutored by, among others, Robert Ogilvie, the Scottish ancient historian, who had a profound influence on his career. Henderson was not British, but as he was born in a former British colony, he held a British passport and was ever conscious of his Scots heritage to which he referred in his lecture, in the presence of the august Scot, Petrie, then aged ninety seven: 'like Professor Petrie I am a Scot, albeit a detribalized one' (1978: 2).

Henderson begins, conventionally, by thanking Raven for leaving him an efficient Department 'which anyone would be proud to head' and for setting it 'on the right path' by making classical courses, especially the languages in the early stages, as attractive as possible (1979: 1). Acknowledging the difficulties of learning Latin and Greek, Henderson obviously does not wish the Department's teachers to sacrifice high standards on the contemporary altar of education for entertainment. *En passant*, he recalls the advice of de Kock, an Afrikaans-speaking classicist and one of the founding *patres* of CASA, formerly an occupant of the chair at Natal: 'We must inspire, as Professor de Kock used to say, but we must also demand – diligence, clear thinking and clear expression' (ibid.: 1).

Unlike Raven, Henderson refuses to offer a defence of the Classics and takes a swipe at the university's bureaucrats present, some of whom would have been involved in the process of 'freezing' and 'unfreezing' posts (including posts in Classics), as the university's finances dictated:

> ... it seemed to me that if the University, despite the academic ice-age through which we are moving, has been farsighted enough to continue this Chair, it would be a case of preaching to the converted (ibid.: 2).

Instead Henderson chooses to give the audience a 'glimpse' of the problems of prejudice and bias ancient historians are obliged to confront in their primary sources, focussing on the career of the attractive Athenian playboy politician, Alcibiades. After skilfully negotiating his way through ambivalent accounts of Alcibiades' career, particularly in Thucydides, Henderson concludes with the following *raison d'être* for the study of ancient history which would have had particular relevance in South Africa, where the constant barrage of propaganda from various state organs, especially the state-controlled radio and television, introduced to the country as late as 1976, constantly required vigilance:

> Alcibiades was at fault as well. He was *too* contemptuous of public opinion, sometimes too clever by half, so that it is not surprising that the ordinary folk of Athens distrusted him. Public opinion, as many a politician has found to his cost, is not without power. Disinterring the truth about a character as colourful as Alcibiades

is not easy. But there is some point in spotting bias and freeing one's mind of prejudice. After all if we cannot detect prejudice in the past, what hope do we have of doing the same in the present where we are far more emotionally involved ? (ibid.: 15)

Although Henderson makes no reference to Oxford or his education there, he does situate himself in the same kind of inclusive-exclusive discourse as Raven. De Kock, Professor of Classics at Natal from 1963-1968 and then first chair of the Classics Department at the Rand Afrikaans University in 1969 (Henderson 1996: 1), is included (the only South African mentioned in the introduction), yet the reference to his Scottish ancestry allies Henderson to Petrie and sets them apart from the predominantly South African audience, a few of whom may have identified with a Scottish heritage (1979: 2).

What puzzled me then and puzzles me now is the notion of a 'detribalized' Scot. At the time 'detribalized' was often used by white English-speaking South Africans to refer, often in a derogatory and patronising way, to educated Blacks who had severed their ethnic ties for an urbane 'Englishness', which resisted the kinds of ethnic identities the homelands were designed to forge.[22] Did Henderson mean, in making the joke, that he perceived himself as an Anglicized Scot, whose education at Balliol had helped him shed his ethnic (and colonial) ties? What did Petrie make of the joke? After sixty-eight years in South Africa, Petrie, who lived in the Victoria Club, then in the centre of the city, appeared still to be very 'tribalized' indeed. An active member of the Caledonian Society, he was an expert on Scots folklore and wrote a much-quoted tribute to 'the Immortal Memory of Robert Burns' on the bicentenary of his birth (Stevens 1959: 10). Interestingly, Stevens regarded Petrie as a 'very great South African' who had never forgotten the 'spiritual ties' which bound him to Scotland (ibid.). Henderson's (probably) innocent joke thus raises the complex question of diasporic identities and the ways in which white English-speakers in South Africa or English-speaking white South Africans juggled various identities simultaneously, foregrounding one or some when necessary, suppressing others when required, often in response to the dictates of power: many Afrikaner nationalists regularly accused English-speaking South Africans of being treacherous *soutpiele*, whose ties with Britain confirmed their suspicions that most English-speakers (especially those at the 'liberal' universities) were 'unpatriotic'. After his brief introduction, Henderson has made it clear that he is: an ancient historian, male, heterosexual, married, a 'detribalized' Scot, a teacher, a student, but not South African, Afrikaans speaking, gay or black!

In the course of his lecture, Henderson had ample opportunity to make his lecture more directly appealing to the audience, the majority of whom were neither classicists nor ancient historians, by referring to wayward South African politicians equally as fickle, but not nearly as attractive, as Alcibiades. In 1978, after the murder of Biko and other atrocities, there was a veritable gallery of rogues he could have used as *exempla*. The one comparison he offers is revealing:

> The following day, Nicias, like Neville Chamberlain after Munich, clutching desperately at the peace he had negotiated, persuaded the Athenians to send ambassadors to Sparta in a last effort to save the tatters of their agreement (ibid.: 9).

It is to relatively distant European history and politics that Henderson refers. If such an analogy were made today in 2010 to an audience at an inaugural of a Professor of Classics on the same campus, it would be meaningless and alienating, as the study of history has been almost entirely Africanized. Thirty years ago, the analogy obviously meant something to the audience or Henderson would not have used it, but it does illustrate how deeply Eurocentric the study and the students of history were in 1978. In 2010, an ancient historian would not necessarily be a Classicist, but could very well be a student of the pre-history of Africa.

The third inaugural lecture I would like to consider is that of Geoffrey Chapman, delivered in 1984. Educated at Trinity College, Oxford, Chapman's doctorate on Aristophanes was completed at the University of South Africa, where Naudé, one of CASA's founding *patres*, was his supervisor. Chapman, who had spent many years in the Classics Department at the Durban campus of the University of Natal (1967-1983), chose for his inaugural the theme of 'Woman in Early Greek Comedy: Fact, Fantasy and Feminism', a version of a paper he had delivered at Harvard in 1982.

On the Pietermaritzburg campus, political activism characterised the early 1980s. By introducing, in 1983, the Universities Amendment

Bill (or 'Quota Bill', as the students named it), which regulated the number of black students who could be admitted to 'white' universities, the government provoked protests against this further violation of academic freedom on the English-speaking 'liberal' campuses (*NUX*, August 1983: 4). Students in Pietermaritzburg marched on the City Hall (*NUX*, February 1984: 7). Further protests against the introduction of a tricameral parliamentary system for Whites, Indians and Coloureds, which had been endorsed by white voters in a national referendum (2 November 1983), took place throughout 1984, stimulated by the formation of the United Democratic Front (20 August 1983), which vigorously rejected the government's 'reforms' (*NUX*, February 1984: 12-13). In the weeks before and after Chapman's inaugural lecture, country-wide protests against the elections for the Indian and Coloured chambers gathered momentum (*NUX*, August 1984: 3, 8-9).

Like Henderson, Chapman, who was also an ancient historian, decides not to offer his audience any defence of Classical Studies, but nevertheless clearly shares Henderson's conviction that a study of the past is essential for an informed interpretation of the present: 'what better way is there to judge our current potential and limitations, than to study *other* cultures past and present?' (1985: 1). Unlike the confidence in the future of the Classics expressed by both Raven and Henderson, Chapman's more muted voice suggests some disquiet about the future of the discipline:

> The attack on Classics for being remote, irrelevant and useless is just part of the tendency of modern materialistic society to believe that nothing is worth having if you cannot sell it for more than it cost you. Before long it will be argued that all education is useless (ibid.: 1-2).

Continuing his criticism of the influence of materialism on society's false assessment of the worth of degrees in the Humanities, he becomes even blunter with a direct allusion to Viljoen (see Chapter 1):

> Not that anybody employs Classicists – the present Minister of Education is an ex-Professor of Classics, which might show that Classicists can have a high market value; and if you glance at some other highly-paid politicians, you might also wonder

whether a high market value has anything to do with quality or ability (ibid.: 2).

Abandoning this intellectual *cul-de-sac*, he turns to his topic for the evening which, he hopes, will contribute 'albeit indirectly, to justifying Classical Studies in the 1980s'. Before this, he adds:

> Meanwhile the Classics Department on the Pietermaritzburg campus will try to keep a high profile internationally, as well as within the University, and hope to make a substantial contribution to the cultural life of the city of Pietermaritzburg (ibid.: 2).

Like Henderson, Chapman tackles the problem of bias and prejudice in ancient sources, especially in dramatic texts (tragedy and comedy), arguing strongly for the view that these texts comment on contemporary social and political issues and are not frozen in the far-off world of myth and fantasy. In particular he explores attitudes towards women in the comedies of Aristophanes and, while he acknowledges that Aristophanes is no proto-feminist, he concludes that Aristophanes had a 'special interest' in the ambiguous position of Athenian women 'inherent in early myth and poetry' (ibid.: 20).

Chapman's inaugural is markedly different from the two delivered in the 1970s. First, it is far more inclusive. There is no reference to his nationality or his Oxford training or to the teaching of Latin and Greek or the upholding of high standards 'in the South African context'. The study of Greece and Rome is regarded as the study of 'other cultures' in the past not, significantly, as the study of *the* other cultures, which dethrones Classics from the assumed centrality of its position in the study of the Humanities.

At the beginning of the academic section of his lecture, he invites the audience to join him on an imaginative tour, which situates the listener within, rather than apart from, the subject of the lecture: 'If you had been a social climber in Athens in about 430 BC, you could have invited Perikles, Sokrates, Herodotos, Thucydides, Euripides, Sophokles and Aristophanes all to the same dinner-party ...' (ibid.: 2-3). Classical Athens is referred to as a 'city about the size of Pietermaritzburg' (ibid.: 3).

Secondly, he uses the term 'Classical Studies' in his introduction, thus positioning the discipline, internationally, alongside Women's Studies, Cultural Studies and Media Studies, as devised in Anglo-American universities, but not (in 1984) in South African universities. The omission of any reference to Latin and Greek in the inaugural also indicates a new identity for the department: courses in Classical Civilization will no longer be lowly *ancillae* fawning on the languages ('proper Classics'), but will constitute the major focus of the department, as the majority of students would soon be enrolled in these courses anyway. Under Chapman's leadership, the Department introduced a course on Women in Antiquity and, when a Women's Studies programme was finally established on the campus in 1989, the Department of Classics was invited to contribute to it and eventually housed and administered the programme (then Gender Studies).

To give an inaugural lecture in Classics in South Africa in 1984, which frankly referred to rape, sexuality, homosexuality and feminism, even in relation to early Greek Comedy, cleverly linked the study of Classics with concerns in other disciplines on the campus and demonstrated how 'modern' the study of Classics could be. In the same year *Acta Classica* featured, *inter alia*, such thrillers as 'Horaz, *Carm.* 1.8' (in German) and a note on 'The Location of Castaballum and Alexander's Route from Mallus to Myriandus', whereas *Akroterion*, more encouragingly, featured a translation into Afrikaans of Semonides' poem *On Women* and news of an 'Homerathon' (a non-stop reading of the *Iliad*) on the Durban campus of the University of Natal.

Finally, Chapman's argument that Greek dramatic texts commented sharply on contemporary political and social realities reflected an important belief which influenced, at this period of increased state repression and interference in the academic freedom of universities, the study of the Humanities at most South African universities (certainly the English-speaking ones): the belief in the importance of contextualization, i.e. rooting intellectual pursuits in the South African context, not because of a trendy flirtation with 'relevance', but because a university education, rather than a mere training, could only be *morally* justifiable, in a country where the majority of people did not have the vote, let alone access to a university education, if it addressed racial, political, social and economic inequities. And a study of the Classics could do that superbly well.[23]

Six years later, in the very year (1990) in which de Klerk announced the unbanning of the ANC, PAC, the Communist Party and various other banned organizations and helped set South Africa on the inexorable road to democracy, Richard Whitaker's inaugural lecture, 'Homer and Orality and Literacy in Ancient Greece' (16 May 1990), was delivered at the University of Cape Town, arguably the premier institution for the study of the Classics in South Africa at the time. In this lecture, like Chapman, Whitaker publicly shifts the traditional discipline in a South African direction and illustrates how contextualised (and Africanised) a study of the Classics can be.

A South African, educated at the Universities of the Witwatersrand, Oxford and St Andrews, Whitaker, in redeploying Maurice Bowra's argument that the *Iliad* and the *Odyssey* were transitional texts, between oral and written traditions, concludes his lecture:

> Finally, I would suggest that we in South Africa are peculiarly well-placed to study this question. A great problem with those texts that are believed to be transitional and that are often compared with one another – such as the *Iliad* and *Odyssey* and medieval epics like *Beowulf* and the French *chansons de geste* – is that they lie so far in the past. We know next to nothing about the circumstances surrounding their composition and so, in debating whether they are 'oral' or 'literate', we inevitably become involved in much question-begging. But in South Africa, at present, transitional texts are being produced all around us, in circumstances that can be precisely controlled. Poets are composing for performance works designed to be heard rather than read; poems which, although they are written, draw heavily on the resources of traditional oral praise poetry. I am thinking especially of the poetry of worker poets such as Qabula, Hlatshwayo and Malange. Study of texts such as these, which can be precisely placed on the oral-literate spectrum, could help to clarify the idea of a 'transitional text' and thus to illuminate the obscure but ever-fascinating Homeric question (1990: 9).

The kind of contextualization which Whitaker suggests conjures up the wraith of Victorian comparative studies and its ordering of the world into Manichean binaries: good/evil; civilized/savage; we/them. If classicists in South Africa were to use the performance poetry of black working-class poets in order to 'illuminate' the Homeric question, how would the poets feel about this? Flattered to be connected to the poetics of canonical texts at the very origins of European literature and the Western tradition? Insulted at being exploited by white academics in search of a subsidy-earning publication in a political environment which would endorse the Africanization of research? Outraged at being considered so 'backward' that the process shaping their form of oral poetry is being compared to that of a poet or collective of poets composing more than two thousand years ago? Comparisons between aspects of Classical civilization and African cultures, especially in South Africa, where the study of the Classics is deeply rooted in unequal power relationships, *can* result in legitimizing the very perceptions they intend to subvert. To explore this further, let us retreat to the cloisters of the neo-Romanesque monastery of Mariannhill, situated in Pinetown, between Durban and Pietermaritzburg.

A German monastic foundation, a priest and comparative studies

While Rhodes was furthering his ambitions in the Cape Colony in 1882, Abbot Franz Pfanner, who had been abbot elect of Maria Stern abbey in Bosnia, arrived in Durban with a party of German-speaking Trappist monks, bought a farm from the Natal Land and Colonization Company and eventually established the monastery of Mariannhill, named after the Virgin Mary and her mother, Anne (Brain 2002: 77-87). By 1887, the very year in which the British annexed Zululand (Giliomee and Mbenga 2008: 168), Mariannhill was considered to be, numerically speaking, the largest abbey in the world (Brain 2002: 81).

The monks, who adhered strictly to the Trappist Rule, which included a vow of silence, manual labour and a Spartan vegetarian diet, not only established an impressive monastic complex, a farm, and a network of dependent stations (some twenty-eight by 1909), but also two schools for disadvantaged black South Africans (one for girls and one for boys), which amalgamated to become St Francis' College in 1909.[24] The school added its first matriculation class in 1936 and, as it was a Roman Catholic school staffed by industrious German nuns, Latin was one of the subjects taught and remained on the curriculum for many years.

In 2009, the school celebrated its centenary. It was and is renowned for its exemplary standards and excellent matriculation results (100% pass rate for the last thirty years), often producing students among the top school-leavers in KwaZulu-Natal. Among its distinguished *alumni* and *alumnae* are Dr B.W. Vilakazi (1906-1947), the great Zulu scholar and literary figure, the first black person to be appointed to the staff of the University of the Witwatersrand, Steve Biko (1946-1977), iconic Black Consciousness leader in the 1970s, murdered by the *apartheid* security forces while in detention under the Terrorism Act, and Dr Matsepe-Casaburri (1937-2009), the first woman and black chair of the SABC and Minister of Communications in South Africa from 1999 until her death.

The first principal of the school was Fr David, otherwise known as Arthur Thomas Bryant (1865-1953), who joined the monastery at eighteen, left the order during the 'monastic crisis' of the late nineteenth century, became an Oblate of Mary Immaculate, and eventually one of South Africa's most respected Zulu linguists and a Research Fellow in Bantu Studies at the University of the Witwatersrand (1920-1923).

Born in England and educated at the Birkbeck Literary and Scientific Institute (later Birkbeck College, University of London), Bryant immigrated to Natal in 1883 and was ordained a priest four years later by the Latin Patriarch of Constantinople in the basilica of St. John Lateran in Rome.[25] As Lugg notes, rather pompously: '... he was privileged to read his first mass on the high altar of St Peter's, a sequence of happenings almost unique for a young priest' (Bryant 1949: ix). Apart from his Zulu-English dictionary, Bryant's *magnum opus* was his magisterial *The Zulu People As They Were Before The White Man Came* (1949), the product of more than fifty years of field work among the Zulus, to whom he dedicates the work: 'A Farewell Tribute to the Zulu People, My Life-long Companions and Friends'.

In the course of *The Zulu People* Bryant reveals not only a sound knowledge of Greek and Roman mythology, but also the Victorian propensity for comparative studies and the Darwinian-inspired hunt for origins. A chapter on the pre-colonial daily life of the Zulus is entitled 'Daily Life in Arcady'; in the chapter, ominously titled 'Mysteries and Myths', Bryant reveals the 'diffusionist' nature of his beliefs about Zulu myth and ritual.

In exploring the myths and rituals associated with Nomkhubulwane, the Zulu 'Corn-and-Sky-Princess', Bryant suggests that she 'bears strong Caucasic features' and may thus be a 'genuine child' of the Mediterranean (1949: 676). The dizzyingly circular argument, influenced by Frazer (and Herodotus!), runs something like this. The Ancient Egyptian branch of the Caucasic 'Mediterranean race' 'made its home along the Nile (where previously a Negro people had lived)' and brought with them a myth of a dying vegetation deity (the corn-god) which 'finally blossomed into the god, Osiris' (ibid.: 675). When the Pelasgian section of this race left North Africa for Greece and Italy, the 'old North African myth went with them' and eventually 'the single corn-and-vine god of the African motherland became cloven in twain, into the corn-goddess, Demeter and Ceres, and the vine-god, Dionysos or Bacchus' (ibid.: 676). If emigrants from the 'old Mediterranean Race of North Africa' went northwards, Bryant asks, surely there is the possibility that some of them went southwards importing into these regions 'something of its blood and customs' (ibid.: 676). It is to her distant ancestors, Demeter and Persephone, that Nomkhubulwane owes her split personality: mother and maiden. *Black Demeter*, rather than *Black Athene*, would perhaps have been a more appropriate title for Bernal's project.

Influenced by the possibilities of Bryant's comparative move, but not by his diffusionism, and by Bernal's work, which had given classicists working in Africa some badly-needed propaganda for their discipline, I wrote an article 'Nomkhubulwane: The Zulu Demeter', published in *Akroterion* in 1990, the same year as Whitaker's inaugural lecture. In his editorial in this edition of the journal, Conradie at Stellenbosch, commenting on a report on the state of the study of Latin and Greek at Dutch universities, wrote:

> Dit beklemtoon weer eens dat die klassikus nooit in 'n toestand van valse gerustheid mag verval nie, maar altyd waaksam moet wees en na nuwe maniere moet soek om sy vak relevant in 'n veranderende wêreld te maak (1990: 45).

This emphazises once again that the classicist must never be lulled into a false sense of security, but must always be alert and in search of new ways of making his discipline relevant in a changing world.

This is precisely why I wrote the article in the rapidly changing South Africa of the early nineties, although I attempted, not very successfully, to situate the traditional comparison (similarities, differences and then some hermeneutic) into a broader feminist framework, exploring the ambiguous position of women within the two patriarchal societies in which the myths of Demeter-Persephone and Nomkhubulwane were shaped. What is interesting for the comparative enterprise in classics in South Africa is the response of students (both black and white) to the article, which is one of the readings set in a course on comparative Greek, Roman and African ritual at the University of KwaZulu-Natal. Although Nomkhubulwane rituals are often in the news, especially since the resurrection of the goddess and her dormant rituals in 1996, and the coupling of this resurrection to the African Renaissance, Zulu moral re-armament and the virginity-testing of young Zulu women, as part of a controversial strategy deployed to fight HIV-AIDS in KwaZulu-Natal, most students know nothing of the goddess's mythology nor of the Victorian prejudices inherent in its transmission.[26] While responses to the article are thus usually positive, some students inevitably ask the question: why did you categorize Nomkhubulwane as the Zulu Demeter? If you claim not to be perpetuating Bryant's diffusionism, why did you not entitle the article 'Demeter: the Greek Nomkhubulwane'? Precisely. In any comparison in South Africa, where one of the poles in the comparison is European and the other African, the author of the comparison, particularly if he is a white classicist, has constantly to interrogate where he positions himself, in order to avoid implicit value-judgments which result in *othering* the African material chosen for the comparative study.

In the next comparative article (1993), published on the eve of South Africa's first democratic elections which ushered in to power the previously banned ANC, I compared ancient Greek and traditional Zulu sacrificial ritual, using the Zulu material to interrogate Burkert's hypothesis about the origins of sacrifice and the first human societies, and concluded with the following:

For what does emerge from any comparative study of this nature is that more questions are raised than answers provided, that insights into one's own discipline, previously muddled or woolly, are honed into shape, that insights into Zulu thought-patterns are provided by the ancient Greeks and vice versa. It is this fact which makes our position as classicists in South Africa exciting; we live amongst people who still sacrifice. I say this not in the spirit of a patronising Victorian ethnographer-classicist who calls in the anthropologist to deal with what Dodds called the 'disagreeably primitive things poking up their heads through the cracks in the fabric of Periclean rationalism', but as one anxious to demonstrate that the study of the Classics in this country can never be irrelevant or pointless. For, as Burkert says, in the pessimistic conclusion to *Homo Necans* wherein he reflects on the breakdown of ritual in the modern world and the consequent unleashing of unchannelled aggression, 'we can only hope that primitivism and violence will not be released unbridled. In any case, our knowledge of the traditions that proved themselves in the past and thus survived in the various experiments of human development should not be lost as we proceed, by trial and error, toward an uncertain future' (1983: 297). In contemporary South Africa, no words could be more apt (Lambert 1993: 311).

In 1993, after the violence of the late 1980s and early 1990s, especially severe in the Pietermaritzburg area in which a civil war raged between supporters of the African National Congress and the Zulu nationalist Inkatha Freedom party, some concern about South Africa's future under black majority rule was understandable. However, to have coupled these fears and linked them to a defence of the study of the Classics in a comparative study which foregrounded the importance of sacrificial ritual in the Zulu tradition, seems to me now to have been unwise. White racist fears about black majority rule in 1993 focussed on the 'unleashing of unchannelled aggression'. Situating the Classics in a stable Eurocentric camp opposed to this seems to me to reflect these fears and undermine the stability of Zulu traditional ritual and its function in channelling such aggression. No South African can, in my opinion, ever claim to be entirely free of racism after centuries of socialization into the kind of antithetical thinking which bedevils it. Thus the 'resistant discourses' generated by English-speaking white South African classicists can, in the process of comparative studies, be as implicit in the rule of oppressive élites as the Afrikaner nationalist voices (see Chapter 1).

87

In subsequent articles, I attempted to answer such criticisms, and the dangerous tendency of comparative studies, referred to by Raven in his inaugural lecture, to import modern values into the ancient world and vice versa, and to resort to 'grand narratives', usually of the Jungian variety, in the conclusions. In comparing aspects of ancient Greek and traditional Zulu medicine, I concluded with the following caveat regarding methodological traps:

> On the one hand, there is the tendency to imagine Zulu impis (or Trobiander islanders) on the plains of Marathon, as scholars attempt to fill in the gaps in the ancient Greek evidence by studying contemporary 'primitive' societies. On the other hand, one can lapse into vague generalities about Jungian archetypes and 'our common humanity reaching across the aeons of time' or deep structures lying silent beneath the bric-à-brac of history. The ancient Greeks were not an African society, although there may well have been African influences on them, mediated through Egypt and Crete, neither were or are the Zulus nascent Greeks, trapped at an earlier stage of evolution. There are, however, enough similarities between the two cultural systems to highlight the differences between them and so clarify their unique distinctiveness. Furthermore, it really is the duty of those of us who teach classics in South Africa to demonstrate that the study of ancient Greek and Roman culture (languages included) is not a colonial irrelevancy or a dilettantish, elitist pastime, but a study which can provide a creative and challenging commentary, often in counterpoint, on the multi-faceted interchange of cultures in contemporary South Africa (Lambert 1995: 79-80).

All the comparative studies I have attempted have been delivered as papers at CASA's biennial conferences and are used as coursework material at the University of KwaZulu-Natal and have, in retrospect, clearly responded to contemporary politics, often to the politics within South African universities or within CASA itself. A later study comparing classical Athenian and traditional African ethics tries to answer some of the objections to the study of the Classics raised by members of the administration at the University of Natal proposing a more aggressive Africanization of the curriculum.

My purpose ... has been to challenge the crass, antithetical mind-set, which pits the Eurocentric against the Afrocentric, and which sees no place in a modern Africanised curriculum for the study of something so essentially European as classical antiquity (Lambert 2000: 41).

Similarly, the conclusion in an article comparing the world of the Greek magical papyri with contemporary African magic as practised in the centre of Pietermaritzburg:

... we classicists have to be very careful that our discipline is not tossed out with what is perceived as European colonialist and imperialist baggage. We can and do offer a richly-layered, inter-disciplinary field of study which breaks down the binaries of European and African and makes what seem strange about Euro-pean societies (however ancient) engagingly familiar (Lambert 2007: 130).

Concluding the comparison of classical Athenian and African ethics with the suggestion that such studies can 'heighten our sensitivity and tolerance, as we attempt to forge a new South Africa, *co-ordinating* change and continuity' (2000: 48) was directed at possible objections from colleagues at a CASA conference at the University of the Western Cape, a former *apartheid* institution for 'Coloureds' with a distin-guished history of resistance to the ideology which created it. It is interesting to note that this comparative discourse becomes more inclu-sive – the 'we' refers to all South Africans, not simply classicists in the audience – the more exclusive the discourse on Africanization becomes.

In Chapter 1, we briefly looked at Haarhoff's comparative studies of the Romans and Afrikaner Boers which were underpinned by a specific political agenda, that is the improvement of relations between Afri-kaans and English-speaking South Africans, which at the time seemed to him (and certainly to General Smuts) to be South Africa's most urgent racial problem. A Classics professor for thirty-five years at an English-speaking university with a liberal tradition (Petrie 1958: 9), Haarhoff was a passionate Afrikaner, whose political beliefs owed a great deal to the influence of Gilbert Murray at Oxford and were thus not directly implicated in Afrikaner nationalist ideology. At the University of Natal

(Pietermaritzburg), I explored how my own identity was shaped by Oxford-educated classicists and by the protest politics of the 1970s. I then examined how the identity of the discipline itself was re-positioned by comparative studies between the ancient Greeks and the Zulu, responding to national and local politics, especially within the universities and the Classical Association. It thus seems to me that the discipline itself has been imbued with a protean identity, which can make and unmake itself in response to political hegemony, precisely because its introduction to the country and its perpetuation were so closely bound up with colonialism, imperialism and then with reactions to these, in the form of Afrikaner nationalism and, in turn, the protesting (and often silently acquiescent) voices of English-speaking liberals. At moments the boundaries or fault-lines between these are subverted by the complex identities of Afrikaner classicists like Hofmeyr and Haarhoff. Comparative studies, however, have influenced not only white South African identities.

When the long-dormant rituals of Nomkhubulwane were being resurrected in the mid-nineties, the Black female *isangoma* (Nomagugu Ngobese), who initiated the project, inspired by an ancestral dream, came to discuss with me the mythology and rituals of Demeter and Persephone and other issues related to mother goddesses in general. To inform her research properly, she travelled around remote parts of KwaZulu-Natal collecting evidence from older women, in particular, about Nomkhubulwane songs and rituals. When the first reconstituted ritual took place in 1996, a much-publicised event which was filmed, I was interested in the tripartite structure of the festival (over three days) and the centrality of the sacrifice (a female animal for a female goddess), for which there was no evidence (pre-colonial or otherwise) at all. On further investigation, it seemed to me that our discussion of classical mother goddesses and rituals such as the Thesmophoria had, perhaps quite unconsciously, found its way into a reconstituted Zulu ritual in the twentieth century. The resuscitation of the Nomkhubulwane rituals seems to me to provide an interesting example of the appropriation of the Classics by a black woman with an Africanist agenda.[27] It is notoriously difficult for white South African males to speak for or about Black men and women and their identities, but I would like to turn, with trepidation, to some exploration of Black South African identities and the Classics.

3

The Classics and Black South
African Identities

I performed in only a few dramas, but I had one memorable role:
that of Creon, the king of Thebes, in Sophocles' *Antigone.*

Nelson Mandela on Robben Island,
in Mandela 1994: 441

Homeland universities

As we noted in Chapter 1, the absurdly-named Extension of University
Education Act (no. 45 of 1959) established university colleges for each
'ethnic' group in keeping with the 'separate but equal' tenet of *apartheid*
ideology. As a course in Latin at tertiary level was still a requirement
for the law degree and Hellenistic Greek was required for the training
of ministers of religion, separate departments of Greek and Latin,
which at times coalesced into Departments of Classics, had to be established at the 'homeland' universities.

As with most master plans which require social engineering, anoma-
lies often occur and the first anomaly was that a university for blacks,
which included Africans, 'Coloureds' and Indians, already existed in the
Eastern Cape – the University of Fort Hare, established in 1916, which
had emerged from the missionary institute of Lovedale, had attracted
black students from all over Africa and was now 'to serve the Xhosa
group' (Behr and MacMillan 1966: 216). The independent homeland of
the Transkei lobbied for the establishment of a university in its capital,
Umtata (now Mthata), and this university came into being in 1976, the
year of the Soweto uprising.

It is with the 'Cinderella of the Classics departments of South Africa'
(Wakerley 1985: 101-2) at the University of Transkei (Unitra) that I
would like to begin this chapter, as this offers an especially interesting

insight into the teaching of Classics by white academics, and identity construction mobilised around language, at 'homeland' universities during the *apartheid* era.

The University of Transkei (Unitra)

In 1983, the British-born and educated Margaret Wakerley, with a doctorate on Callimachus from London University, became head of a Department of Classics (Latin, Greek and Classical Culture) at Unitra where previously only Latin had been taught for the purposes of the law degree. At CASA's first colloquium on the teaching of the classical languages at tertiary level in 1982, Wakerley gave a paper on how she taught Latin to isiXhosa-speaking law students at the university, outlining the difficulties encountered by many teaching Latin 'as a service course': evening classes after work, very little time for revision, and students with a limited knowledge of English.

Describing herself as a *quadrata* ('an old-fashioned square') and 'no longer a dewy-eyed enthusiast for the cause of Latin', Wakerley rejects 'with-it fancy methods' in favour of a practical course, derived from that offered at the University of Durban-Westville, which will get the job done 'hopefully without tears or boredom' (1982: 98). To achieve this, she gives detailed examples of how she has adapted her knowledge of isiZulu (an Nguni language closely related to isiXhosa) in order to teach Latin more effectively to students who know little English. She begins with this rationale:

> There are many advantages in having a working knowledge of their language. It enables one to cope with their mistakes, one knows *why* they make them, not just *what* they do, and if one bypasses the *tertium quid* of English and explains the error in terms of their own grammar, the intelligent ones, at least, will not make the same mistake again (ibid.: 99).

Acknowledging that there is no relationship between isiXhosa and Latin, Wakerley believes that what she calls the 'psychology of speech is the same' and that 'the psychological effect of a lecturer's knowing their language is very good' (ibid.: 99). Providing an extensive list of 'points of contact' between Latin and isiXhosa/isiZulu, Wakerley concludes:

They seem to have the same trouble with Latin endings as English speakers do, in spite of the fact that they are used to changing suffixes and prefixes in Xhosa (is this because they are learning through English?). Most of them are not case-conscious, and their expertise in Xhosa, having been imbibed subliminally with their mother's milk, is of little help. The few clever ones pick up the idea at once and make few mistakes, but the others flounder on regardless! (ibid.: 100).

Despite Wakerley's considerable efforts to familiarise herself with the language of her students, she perpetuates a variant of the inclusive-exclusive discourse we examined in Chapter 2. The constant use of 'they' and 'them' conjures up the *apartheid* educationalist convinced that he knows what kind of education is best for 'them'; patronising condescension – 'the few clever ones' – is interlaced with perceptions of the happy natives 'imbibing' language along with their mother's milk and apparently incapable of reflecting on the process of language acquisition. It is Wakerley and her Latin course which are to rescue black Transkeians from the primitive breast. Beneath the surface of Wakerley's article there lurks the kind of racism produced by a system in which the process of *othering* is inescapable: Wakerley refers to her students as 'deficient in the basic elements of European culture' (1982: 97). In her comments on the psychology of using the students' home language, Wakerley identifies precisely what Francois Smuts referred to, in relation to the teaching of the Classics to Afrikaans-speakers through the medium of English: the reluctance of the students to relate to a discipline taught in the language of the coloniser and oppressor (see Chapter 1).

I have not been able to find any evidence of an isiXhosa-speaking student's reaction to Wakerley's Latin classes, but she herself gives some indication of student response in a 'follow-up' article published in *Akroterion* in 1985. Undergoing a Damascus-style conversion, Wakerley describes how she decides to design her own Latin course

geared to the needs of *our* students, i.e. black Transkeians mostly, with no Latin and little educational background, reading Law and needing Latin only because the Statute demands it, moreover, working under conditions of exceptional difficulty (1985: 101).

Abandoning the old-fashioned methods and textbooks 'designed for English children in English schools, lost in the mists of time' (ibid.: 100), she fashions, from day to day, a language course beginning with the vocabulary required for the study of a selection of legal texts. In contrast to the world-weary cynicism expressed in the first article, an enthused Wakerley notes that the students now 'actually like Latin':

> They are enthusiastic, pursue me for homework they have missed and some even come to extra tutorials. One student, who had failed the previous year in the old course, told me he found the new one 'hard, but interesting' (ibid.: 101).

Furthermore, Wakerley refers to the teaching of Greek 'motivated by the needs of the Department of Religious and Biblical Studies' (ibid.: 101) and comments on the introduction of a Classical Culture course with two students, the black headmaster of a local school, 'who did Latin up to Matric in the good old days and loves it', and a 'young white man' (ibid.).

Despite Wakerley's rediscovered enthusiasm for Latin teaching and the apparently positive response of some of her students, the same exclusive discourse, evident in the first article, resurfaces. Commenting on the reading of some of Phaedrus' fables, which she turned into Latin prose and whose 'subject-matter was not the most interesting for them', Wakerley remarks:

> One great drawback in our students is what appears to be a lack of imagination, so that they cannot make the leap from fact to fiction – they know all the words in a sentence, but stare blankly at them, unable to shape them into a meaning. (This could, of course, be due to the fact that English is not their own language.) (ibid.: 102)

Despite her claims to be rid of English textbooks, she admits that she uses stories from 'an ancient reading book from England, *the Friday afternoon Latin book*' (ibid.: 102). The course is clearly taught exclusively in English: the isiXhosa analogies seem to have been abandoned.

Wakerley's reference to the black headmaster who 'did Latin up to Matric in the good old days and loves it', and who wanted to read Latin at the university not for law purposes, but out of interest (ibid.: 101), hints at the appropriation of the classical tradition among the black community, ignored by the founding *patres* of CASA and most of its regional branches, with the exception of the Western Cape.[1] The head-master is referred to as 'middle-aged' (ibid.: 103): one thus assumes that the 'good old days' refer to pre-*apartheid* education, most likely in a mission school. Furthermore, Wakerley's reference to the 'young white man' in her Classical Culture class indicates that Unitra was (by 1984 at any rate) an 'open' university, not restricted to black isiXhosa-speak-ers. Fissures in the *apartheid* masterplan had already begun to appear. Wakerley bleakly concludes:

> I cannot say what would have happened in the second year of their [Latin] course, as it has been interrupted by the troubles at the University and even if the situation is normal for the rest of the year, it is going to be very difficult to get through the syllabus in time for exams in November (ibid.: 102).

With this allusion, which foregrounds the difficulties of teaching at the 'homeland' universities during the 1980s, Wakerley refers to the politi-cal unrest spawned by the introduction of the tricameral parliamentary system (for whites, 'coloureds' and Indians) in 1984 (see Chapter 2), unrest which resulted in 1985, after the murder of the 'Cradock Four' by the security police, in the proclamation of yet another state of emergency, and further state repression.

A decade later (1994), when Nelson Mandela had been elected as South Africa's first democratically elected president, Jan Els, teaching at the University of Fort Hare, offers a more sophisticated discussion of the problems of teaching the Classics to black South Africans.

An Afrikaner, educated at Potchefstroom University, Els posits a 'significant cleavage' between African and Western world-views and life views (1994: 164), and believes that a course in Classical Culture cannot avoid being 'Eurocentric in nature' (ibid.: 166). Els suggests that 'paral-lels, similarities, affinities and resemblances with the present SA could be stressed' (ibid.: 166), but rejects looking at Afro-Asiatic influences ('à la Black Athena') or links with Roman Africa as, because of 'their remoteness in time and space', these topics 'do not really make the course more indigenous in the eyes of the students' (ibid.: 166). Believing that a Nigerian *Oedipus* 'qualifies much better', presumably to make the course 'more indigenous', he regrets that black South African writers have not yet appropriated the classical tradition (ibid.: 166).

Turning explicitly to the comparative studies of Graeco-Roman and African religious myth, ritual and social custom, explored in Chapter 2, he considers such studies 'interesting and valuable', but impossible to accommodate in an introductory course on Classical Culture. Furthermore, he elaborates on this opinion by stating that the 'value and relevance' of a Classical Culture course in the present South Africa does not depend 'on the ability to find a proliferation of direct connections, explicit influences and analogies or even on making meaningful comparisons':

> I do not think that it is necessary to search frantically for such items to justify the course or to Africanise it to the extent of artificiality (ibid.: 166-7).

So why, in Els's opinion, should black South Africans study the Classics in a university in which, he concedes, the study of the Classics is not rated very highly precisely because such study is perceived as 'having no immediate vocational value' (ibid.: 164)?

The reasons Els offers for a study of the Classics are an interesting blend of the political language of the new South Africa and familiar well-trodden arguments related to the 'extension of intellectual and cultural horizons' (ibid.: 165). Els argues that the opening up of the 'classical heritage' will provide 'a new avenue for a society in transition' (ibid.: 164). Topics in Classical Culture should also 'deal with problems that are still current': e.g. democracy, reform, control of political power, land distribution, violence, clash and fusion of different cultures, literary and artistic theory, values in education (ibid.: 165-6). To be avoided at all costs is a 'paternalistic attitude of the superiority of Classical or Western culture, as if it is the canonical measure of all things, and a Graeco-Roman puristic view' (ibid.: 167).

Amidst the familiar arguments in support of a study of the Classics at an all-black university in the 'new' South Africa, are ones relating to broad 'cultural enrichment' and a 'better insight' into civilizations 'whose expectations, values and attitudes reflect many of our own' (ibid.: 165). Interestingly, Els believes that understanding of the modern world can be enhanced by 'comparing it with a different cultural milieu, thereby developing self-knowledge, critical awareness and tolerance' (ibid.: 165). In support of his arguments, Els summons up the *manes* of both Haarhoff and Viljoen. The former's words, penned in 1959, are cited with approval:

> We must try and see how far man at a particular point has succeeded in being civilized, stumbling along in his blinded way and obsessed with his 'homesickness for the mud', as the French say (ibid.: 167).

Although more thoughtful and more sensitive to the needs of his students than Wakerley, Els reveals that his discourse is also shot through with similar contradictions. His unease about comparisons and parallels results in a curiously circular argument which undermines his position: comparisons do not justify the study of Classics nor 'Africanise it', but comparison between the students' world and a different 'cultural milieu' develops the humane values one would wish to nurture in the 'new' South Africa. Els suggests dealing with topics in antiquity which resonate, keenly, with contemporary South Africa (e.g. land distribution and control of political power), but is worried about the dangers of 'slanting': 'during the height of violence in SA one could put e.g. the Peloponnesian War on a Procrustean bed' (ibid.: 166). It is this fear which finds him retreating into the very Eurocentricity which he argues must be avoided. The argument that a study of the Classics should result in 'better' insight into 'our' expectations, values and attitudes makes one wonder to whom 'our' really refers. The citation from Haarhoff clinches it: it is Western civilization, after all, which, in the tradition of Victorian classicists and missionaries, provides the best example of the evolutionary climb from primitivism to civilization. Positive endorsement of Haarhoff's use of the French expression *la nostalgie de la boue* seems to me to be especially insensitive: apart from the Calvinism which underpins Haarhoff's reasons for studying the Classics – the grace of the Classics will redeem the savage brute from his fallen nature – black students at Fort Hare, 'many of whom come from homes where there are no or only a few books' (ibid.: 164), are clearly perceived as among the fallen who have stumbled along their blinded way. Finally, if study of the Black Athena hypothesis or of the links with Roman Africa does not make the course 'more indigenous' in the students' eyes, due to their 'remoteness in time and space', one wonders how Els's alternative suggestions, which do not make the study of Classical Culture any less remote in time and space, could possibly have any validity at all.

Both Wakerley and Els illustrate the minefield of ambiguities through which white classicists, English- and Afrikaans-speaking, attempt to navigate as they are confronted by black South African students, who need to be convinced of the value and relevance of a study of the Classics, in a context where political decolonization has not necessarily resulted in decolonization of the mind. In their respective contexts, both realise that the identity of the discipline itself has to be refashioned and make enlightened suggestions about how this can be achieved, yet, in the process, both resort to clichéd Victorian arguments for the study of the Classics, which perpetuate the kind of crass *othering* they intend to obviate.

The good old days

One of Els's predecessors at the University of Fort Hare, established as the South African Native College in 1916 with eventual government approval (Higgs 1997: 34), was D.D.T. Jabavu, for twenty years the only black member of the teaching staff, who was formally awarded the title of professor (of Bantu Studies) in 1942 (ibid.: 49). By the 1940s 'Fort Hare had become the premier college for Africans in southern Africa, and was drawing students from throughout the region' (ibid.: 49). In his autobiography, *Long Walk to Freedom* (1994), Nelson Mandela, who was taught anthropology by Jabavu at Fort Hare, confirms this, describing the university as

> a beacon for African scholars from all over Southern, Central and Eastern Africa. For young black South Africans like myself, it was Oxford and Cambridge, Harvard and Yale rolled into one (1994: 41).[2]

A list of some of its alumni, which reads like a *Who's Who* of southern African political and intellectual history, illustrates the significant role Fort Hare played in the development of African nationalism and, later,

Black Consciousness: Nelson Mandela (1940), Oliver Tambo (1941), Robert Sobukwe (1946), Govan Mbeki (1937), Dennis Brutus (1947), Robert Mugabe (1951) (de Kock 1996: 63).

Educated at the Lovedale Missionary Institution, to give it its full name, the African Training Institute (Colwyn Bay, Wales), because Dale College in King William's Town refused to admit him, the University of London and the University of Birmingham (Higgs 1997: 14-31), Jabavu began his career at Fort Hare teaching Latin to classes of students, who recalled his inspirational teaching of the subject many years later:

> Students who had studied Latin with him fifty years previously could still quote Latin phrases almost thirty years after his death, and delighted in mimicking the stutter that plagued him when he got excited (ibid.: 37).[3]

Why Jabavu was teaching Latin at South Africa's first 'native' university college recalls the debate about the implications of teaching the Classics to Africans which raged at Lovedale in the late nineteenth century, led to the resignation of the first principal (William Govan), involved Jabavu's well-known father (John Tengo Jabavu) and, most importantly, reached to the heart of the vexed question of colonial education and African identities.

Established by the Glasgow Missionary Society in 1824, Lovedale became in 1841 a seminary providing a high school education for Africans and the children of white missionaries (Burchell 1976: 60). Because of its press, operational on its former site as early as 1826, and responsible, for instance, for the publication of the first grammar of an indigenous South African language, Lovedale developed into what was for many years 'the largest and most influential missionary educational institution in the country' (de Kock 1996: 69).

De Kock has identified three phases in Lovedale's history in the nineteenth century: the first, under the Reverend Govan, which aimed at offering blacks an education equal to that available to whites, including instruction in Greek and Latin; the second, under James Stewart (1870-1905), which shifted Lovedale's educational focus from the academic to the vocational, believing, rather like Verwoerd, that there was really no place for the African in European society above certain levels of labour; and the third, also during Stewart's principalship, during which interrogation of what was perceived as 'missionary paternalism' resulted in the secession of Lovedale-trained black ministers from the Lovedale congregation (1996: 70-1).

In response to the Grey Plan of the 1850s, which explicitly linked industrial education in the Cape Colony with the civilization of the 'barbarians', vocational training had been initiated at Lovedale, although Govan emphasized the importance of the academic curriculum, which included the classics, mathematics, logic and theology (ibid.: 72). Inevitably, tensions between the two positions (the academic versus the vocational) developed, and the teaching of Greek and Latin became the precise focus of them. The ensuing dispute, between Govan and his successor, Stewart, resulted in submissions to the Free Church of Scotland Foreign Missions Committee, which decided in favour of Stewart, pronouncing that the classical languages 'should be sacrificed if they stand in the way of the pupils acquiring a thorough understanding of English' (Shepherd 1941: 160). Govan resigned and Stewart became the next principal.

During Stewart's long and, from the point of view of colonial aspirations for the 'natives', successful principalship, John Tengo Jabavu, D.D.T. Jabavu's father, who was editor of the Lovedale-controlled newspaper *Isigidimi Sama Xosa* ('The Xhosa Messenger'), was rebuked by the principal for his political comment, which criticised the prime minister and governor of the Cape, and commented on elections and on parliamentarians who depended on African votes (De Kock 1996: 117). In 1884, John Tengo Jabavu resigned his editorship and began to publish his own newspaper, *Imvo Zabantsundu* ('Native Opinion'), with the financial backing of white 'liberal' Cape politicians such as Rose-Innes and his supporters. This was the 'first black-owned and edited newspaper in any South African African language' (Giliomee and Mbenga 2008: 180).

Stewart's public utterances at the time clearly reveal his belief in the retardation of African civilization and hence the impossibility of equality for black South Africans (de Kock 1996: 89). This extended to the teaching of Latin and Greek as well. In an undated pamphlet, entitled 'On Native Education – South Africa', Stewart wrote:

Educational equality is probably looked at as a step to further equality. There is such an idea existing among a small and not very satisfactory class. Hence there is a strong desire, almost amounting to a craze, for Latin and Greek among a few, though the amount of knowledge gained of such subjects is, of course, useless (quoted in de Kock 1996: 90).

In the very first edition of *Imvo* (1884), which contained columns in isiXhosa and English, John Tengo Jabavu, defending the role of an independent black newspaper which mediated between the 'aboriginal population' and the 'ruling power', touched directly on the question of black identities and their relationship to colonialist discourses:

> ... Students of the Native Question, then, may well rejoice at living to see a regular organ of native opinion set up. In that organ they will, no doubt, not only expect 'to see themselves as others see them', but also to see us as we see ourselves (in de Kock 1996: 110).[4]

Two months later, in January 1885, *Imvo* published the presidential address of Elijah Makiwane, head of the Native Educational Association, which addressed the Lovedale principal's well-publicised views on the impossibility of equality between Europeans and Africans. In a penetrating analysis of this speech, de Kock argues that Makiwane appears to acknowledge English cultural superiority and then undermines this racist assumption by challenging the stereotyping on which it is based (1996: 117-20).

In the February issue of the same year, *Imvo* published part two of Makiwane's address, which extolled the virtues of the Great Queen as Mother of all, seeming to imply some dissonance between the symbol of the queen as the mother of equality and justice, and the work of the queen's officials in the colonies, devoid of both (ibid.: 120-1). These articles resulted in an editorial spat with Lovedale's *Isigidimi*, to which John Tengo Jabavu eloquently contributed (ibid.: 122).

It is in the context of the 'equality' controversy that the subject of 'natives' studying the Classics was again raised by Jabavu senior, who had taught elementary Latin at Lovedale, in the pages of *Imvo* (May 1885), in direct response to a comment in the *Christian Express* (formerly the *Kaffir Express*) that the teaching of Classics to Africans at Lovedale had done no good at all, but had produced 'positive evil' (ibid.: 125):

> With all due respect to the worthy and esteemed Principal of Lovedale Institution, we ask, what positive evil have classics produced to natives trained at Lovedale? ... The native lads are complaining loudly to their parents and guardians that they do not enjoy the advantages now in the Lovedale classes that the European lads enjoy ... They cannot understand why the difference is being made ... The Europeans are given other subjects to study, but Natives are prohibited, even when they express a desire to study those subjects. These are classical studies. The parents know nothing of Latin and Greek, but would like to be informed as to why the difference is made. The *Express* has partially told us the reason for this. It does not arise from unwillingness to see natives enjoying the same advantages as the white race, but in the native mind classics produce positive evil! (in de Kock 1996: 125).

Jabavu then challenges the Lovedale authorities head-on and requests lists of African young men who studied the Classics there and 'who are now a disgrace to Lovedale and a failure' and of students who did not read the Classics there and are 'now a credit to the Institution and a success in the country' (ibid.: 126). He concludes with a singularly important point: denial of the study of the Classics to students at Lovedale automatically excludes them from sitting for the entrance examinations of the University of the Cape of Good Hope, for which Latin was still a compulsory subject (ibid.: 126), and incidentally, from the legal and medical professions both of which then required a qualification in Latin (Higgs 1997: 16). Lovedale, of course, failed to provide the lists, but Jabavu published in *Imvo* (June 1885) a letter from 'Lovedalian' of Kimberley, who provided 'an impressive list of leading African clergymen, translators, schoolmasters and others who had taken classics at Lovedale' (de Kock 1994: 74) and repeatedly asked the question, after citing each group, what evil or failure had been committed by these distinguished *alumni*. The correspondent from Kimberley ended with a rhetorical flourish, revealing his training in moral philosophy received at Lovedale: preventing students from studying the Classics at Lovedale was 'an interference with the principle of free will' (ibid.: 74).

After another round fired by Lovedale, in the form of a letter to *Imvo* written by none other than John Knox Bokwe, then Stewart's personal assistant at Lovedale, John Tengo Jabavu himself entered the fray again in support of Lovedalian's list of successes (de Kock 1994: 74-5).

Eventually, the *Christian Express*, edited by Stewart, took up the cudgel on behalf of his position in an editorial which sarcastically referred to *Imvo* as the 'great champion of classical education for natives, and also of higher education as it understands that question' (August 1885). The article challenged Jabavu to inform his 'native' readers – 'that not very large portion of the native people who read':

> *Tell them this – that the life and death question of the native people in this country now, is not classics or even politics – but industry;* that the foothold the natives will be able to maintain in this country depends almost entirely on the habit of steady conscientious work; and that is of more consequence for them to understand this, than to be able to read all the lore of the ancients (ibid.: 127).

Jabavu's reply (August 1885) cleverly cuts to the heart of the matter (equal education for all) and draws the attention of the editor of the *Christian Express* to the (unintentional, of course) errors made in the editorial:

> It does not follow because we are thorough believers in the doctrine that as a rule, the more a man is educated the better fitted he is for whatever post it may please God to call him, we are therefore 'champions of classical education for natives', and so forth. In connection with the educational controversy ... we have taken our stand against those who were understood to imply, if not to suggest that 'conscience has a colour and quality of work a hue' and who were for the equipping of the Native for the future in such a manner as to lead one to believe that the contrary were the fact. So minded then, we have merely claimed for our people 'a fair field and no favour' in the matter of classical or higher education (ibid.: 127-8).

Jabavu's retort is redolent with the language of the Cape liberal tradition and its belief in 'equal rights for all civilized men' enshrined in the Cape constitution of 1853 and in the non-racial franchise (Higgs 1997: 22), shaped by English liberalism of the period.

What is extremely important about the 'classics debate' is that a black intellectual in the Cape Colony in the late nineteenth century explicitly connects the study of Greek and Latin with the acquisition of civilization and with equality of access to education, and with access to political power – the colonial bureaucracy, university education and thence professions such as law and medicine. In a context where the study of the classics was positioned as essential to the exercise of imperialist power, denial of this study to Africans logically implied that they were condemned to be eternal 'hewers of wood and carriers of water', marginalised by the very civilization to which they were encouraged to aspire. In the first edition of *Imvo*, Jabavu had argued that 'students of the Native Question' would find an 'organ' of 'native opinion' interesting for two reasons: they (i.e. the whites) could expect 'to see themselves as others see them' and see 'us as we see ourselves'. For the British colonials, and especially the missionaries at Lovedale, so conscientiously involved in the process of transforming the 'native' into good Christian gentlemen, Jabavu's newspaper would reflect their process of *othering* back to them and would also reveal how African identities could be constructed by Africans, within and apart from imperialist discourses. Jabavu had appropriated the language, education and politics of the conqueror, yet when he demonstrated how he wished to exercise freedom of *choice*, in relation to classical education, a freedom essential to the very notion of liberalism, the empire struck back because he seemed not to have internalised the subservient identity constructed for him. Perhaps it was precisely this which the writer in the *Christian Express* perceived as being the 'positive evil' which the study of the Classics wrought on the 'native mind'. The ambiguous inclusive-exclusive discourse discussed previously is deeply embedded in the imperialist 'message'.

Almost exactly a century after the 'classics debate' in 1885, Els notes that his students at the University of Fort Hare, across the river from Lovedale, do not rate the study of the Classics highly because they have 'no immediate vocational value', thus demonstrating that once the study of Classics is cut adrift from the centres of political and economic power, especially from professions such as law and medicine, black South Africans resort to the kind of argument used by the white colonialists at Lovedale in the nineteenth century. Wakerley's flawed attempts to 'sell' Latin to her isiXhosa-speaking students at the University of the Transkei, especially her attempts to bridge the language divide, resonate with another aspect of the 'classics debate' at Lovedale in the nineteenth century: the need to acquire a sound knowledge of English.

In 1901, Hunter, the editor of the *Christian Express*, contributed to the debate by remarking that African students at Lovedale, instead of desiring to learn Greek and Latin, should learn English properly before 'lumbering their minds with a superficial knowledge of one or two dead languages' (in Higgs 1997: 17).

The context of this contribution to the debate is revealing. John Tengo Jabavu's son had been rejected by Dale College, thus exposing the *de facto* segregation which existed in Cape Schools; a debate in the local English press ensued; the editor of *Izwi Labantu* ('The Voice of the People'), opposed to Jabavu because of his support for the Afrikaners in the South African War (1899-1902), came out on his side on this occasion 'for going to the root of the question and exposing the rottenness of the European position' and protested that, because higher education in the Cape was clearly not for Africans, they had to go to the United States (Higgs 1997: 16).[5]

Hunter then replies to *Izwi*, noting that few students take the matriculation course at Lovedale anyway, before making the remarks about the necessity to master English. In the context of the South African War, in which (by 1902) more than 200,000 British troops were involved (Giliomee and Mbenga 2008: 215), Hunter's remarks about the necessity to 'master' English smack of wartime jingoism and 'exposes the rottenness of the European position' and its treacherous ambiguity: what would be the point of a 'mastery' of English, if this led down a political, social and cultural *cul-de-sac*? What was the point of a liberal constitution with a non-racial franchise, if state schools practised *de facto* segregation? What was the point of an 'industrial, vocational' education if there was 'the ever-present fear that education might transform the African into a successful competitor against the Whites' (Burchell 1976: 61)?

Significantly, in the same year as Hunter's article (1901), John Tengo Jabavu's *Imvo* was banned by the Cape government because of its perceived pro-Boer position. The empire had effectively silenced a voice which interrogated and exposed the rottenness at its core. In Chapter 1, we noted how the study of the Classics and the language in which it was taught was inextricably bound up with the formation of Afrikaner identity. Hunter's opposition between English and the Classics suggests that, unlike white Afrikaners, blacks should not be given the educational and political space to contest the teaching of the classics in a language not their own. Imperialist racism constitutes the 'rottenness of the European position'. What neither Hunter nor Wakerley considers is whether a study of the classical languages has a positive influence on the learning of English: such a move would presumably be too much for the 'native mind'.

The 'Classics debate' at Zonnebloem

If Lovedale was the premier institution for black education in the Cape Colony in the nineteenth and early twentieth centuries, Zonnebloem Native College, an Anglican foundation, situated on the edge of District Six in Cape Town, was regarded as almost its equal. Established in 1858 by Sir George Grey, the Governor of the Colony, and Robert Gray, the Anglican Bishop of Cape Town, the school embodied the co-operation of church and state in what Christison terms the 'ideological disarmament' of the sons of rebellious black chiefs from the troubled periphery of the colony (the Eastern Cape) (2007: 205-6).

Inevitably, however, tensions developed between Grey's industrial educational ideas and the beliefs of the Bishop in the traditional liberal education of a Christian gentleman, which included the Classics and aimed at the moral, spiritual and intellectual 'transformation' of the 'native'. The college relied heavily on the colonial government subsidy to survive and this subsidy was tied to the industrial training provided; the Bishop, however, in whose house (Bishop's Court) the school first began, had to use his influence with various governors in order to ensure that the academic programme (Latin and Greek included) was continued, without the loss of the subsidy (ibid.: 208). In this conflict between church and state, the church seems to have had the upper hand, precisely because the Bishop exploited the ambiguous 'message' of empire discussed previously.

In 1884, more than a decade after the death of Bishop Gray, Canon

Peters, who was the head teacher and taught a very full programme of, inter alia, Greek, Latin, Mathematics and Philosophy, wrote in the college report:

> We use [classical languages] simply as instruments; we know of no better way of making a boy think – of making him able to understand the thoughts of others and to express his own – than by making him translate from one language to another, and for this purpose no languages are so well adapted as those of Greece and Rome (in Christison 2007: 210).

Addressing the objections of those who believed that the study of the Classics was not intended for those 'who are to occupy the lower positions of life', Peters dismissed these objections as 'founded upon a wrong conception of the nature of education and of the duty of the educator':

> Education is the training of the person in mind and body, or in the more accurate division of our being, body and soul and spirit. It is the making of the most of him (in Christison 2007: 560).

One of Peters' students at Zonnebloem at this time was the 'coloured' poet and journalist, Robert Grendon (*c.* 1867-1949), son of an Irish father and a Herero mother, who studied both Greek and Latin and successfully wrote the matriculation examinations of the Cape Colony in 1889.[6]

Qualifying as a teacher, Grendon's first post was at the Anglican St Alban's Native Training College and Industrial School in Pietermaritzburg in the Colony of Natal, where he became involved with the teaching of printing (one of the trades offered along with carpentry, gardening and house work), and with the publication of an isiZulu-English newspaper (*Inkanyiso yase Natal*, 'Enlightener of Natal'), which became a mouthpiece for Funamalungelo (Christison 2007: 245-7), the first African political organization in Natal (ibid.: 245-8).

Grendon's sojourn at St Alban's, closed by the colonial government after 1896, precisely because of the competition provided for white artisans by the skilled blacks the school produced, prepared him for his subsequent career as a journalist and a fighter for black rights. In particular, his editorship of the English columns of John Langalibalele Dube's newspaper, *Ilanga lase Natal* ('Natal's Sun') (1904-1905), and of *Abantu-Batho* ('People') in Johannesburg (1915-1916), connect him with the formative years of black nationalism in South Africa and with the political movement which was to become the African National Congress (ibid.: 249-50).[7]

Grendon's literary output includes the major epic poem *Paul Kruger's Dream* (4,750 lines), first published in full in Pietermaritzburg in 1902, and provocatively subtitled 'The Struggle for Supremacy in South Africa between Boer and Briton, or the overthrow of "Corruption", "Falsehood", "Tyranny", "Wrong" and the triumph of "Justice", "Truth", "Liberty", "Right" '. Rooted in his experiences as a driver of a forge-wagon for the British forces during the South African War (1899-1902), Grendon's poetic account of the war and its genesis, from the perspective of the defeated Boer president, draws on the apparatus of Vergilian and Miltonic epic, including the gods Jove, Phoebus and Mars, the goddess *Fortuna*, and the high-flown language and imagery of classical epic (Christison 2007: 397-483). Intertextual references to classical and English literature abound, including references to Homer's *Iliad* and *Odyssey* and Victorian English poetry indebted to them. As the subtitle of the epic suggests, Grendon associates the Boers and their atrocities committed against Africans, from the time of van Riebeeck, whose wraith makes a dramatic appearance in the poem, with 'corruption, falsehood, tyranny and wrong', and the British with 'justice, truth, liberty and right'.[8]

From the opening invocation to Britannia, who purges 'this polluted Boer domain', and her re-appearance at the end where she delivers an elegy over Cecil Rhodes, extolling his achievements and his apparent freedom from Kruger-style racial prejudice, it is clear that Grendon, at this stage of his life, had internalised the imperialist propaganda meted out to him during his years at Zonnebloem. Identifying himself as black, Grendon was to write the following in *Ilanga* two years after the war (1904):

We [blacks] are not British in blood though British subjects loyal to the core; and anything insulting to British honour must of necessity touch us as well, and cause us uneasiness (in Christison 2007: 207).

3. The Classics and Black South African Identities

Some months later, while Grendon was headmaster of the Zulu Christian Industrial School (Ohlange College) near Durban, during the absence of the renowned John Dube in the United States, he wrote, in the same newspaper, that black parents should

> copy the poverty-stricken [ancient] Greek parent who with small resources flinches not to sacrifice all other interests in order that he might educate a daughter or son' and that black students should 'copy in self-denial the Greek youth who to obtain an education deems it no disgrace and no shame to engage in any work even the lowest and the most mean' (ibid.: 523).

Grendon's somewhat romanticised (and historically inaccurate) view of ancient Greek education and the 'sacrifices' involved in accessing it suggests that the kind of Classics taught at Zonnebloem was tainted with the Protestant work ethic, Victorian denial and features of the 'education versus vocational training debate' encountered at Lovedale.

In the post-war period, Grendon obviously became disillusioned with the way in which discriminatory British 'justice' was implemented in Natal (ibid.: 586-7) and with the fact that British victory in the South African War had not 'purged the Boer domain' of racist cruelties. In particular, British intentions to partition Swaziland 'in a way that greatly favoured the white minority' (ibid.: 737) and the Natives' Land Act of 1913, passed after the Union of South Africa came into being, deepened his sense of outrage at white duplicity and British complicity in racism, despite Britannia's liberal rhetoric. However, before giving a lecture in Johannesburg in 1916, under the auspices of the International Socialist League, Grendon prefaced his lecture, entitled 'Links between the White and the Black', with a request to the chairman of the meeting that an expression of sympathy be recorded for the recent death of Lord Kitchener (ibid.: 815-16). Grendon's loyalty to the Empire and his identity as a British subject ran very deep indeed.

Grendon's classical education and his socialization into 'Englishness' at Zonnebloem seems to have produced an uneasy identity, characteristic of many 'coloured' South Africans of this and later periods. He identifies himself as black; the British he so admired classified him as 'coloured', hence his role as a wagon driver in the South African War because a 'non-white' could not carry arms; the Johannesburg *Star* (1916) classified him as a 'scholarly and cultured Swazi' (ibid.: 816), thus resorting to the kind of ethnic categorization which characterized the *apartheid* years. His study of classical literature, particularly the Vergil he read at Zonnebloem, obviously shaped his identity as a poet, but the style he employs and his romanticization of the ancient Greeks situate him directly in the tradition of late Victorian discourse about the classics. His Swedenborgianism too, which conceptualises the world in Manichaean polarities, also reflects imperialist discourses about civilization and savagery (white/black, good/evil) in the late nineteenth century. The ambivalence of his racial identity intersects with the ambivalence of the empire's message about 'justice', 'liberty' and 'truth'. These 'grand narratives' of empire are constantly undermined by his experiences of British colonial rule in daily practice, as his many newspaper articles attest. As was the case with the Jabavus, Grendon's classical education, which was embedded in a treacherously idealistic view of British intentions in Africa, ultimately prepared him for an intellectual no-man's-land, forever betwixt and between, neither white nor black, at the whim of *Fortuna* disguised as Britannia.

Lovedale's distinguished communist

In April 1993, Martin Thembisile ('Chris') Hani (b. 1942) was assassinated by white right-wing extremists from the Afrikaner Weerstandsbeweging (Afrikaner Resistance Movement), intent on derailing the negotiations which eventually resulted in South Africa's first democratic election in 1994. The tension in the country was palpable and unbearable. I recall at the time taking an Australian visitor to the centre of the city where I live (Pietermaritzburg); we had to make our way through the broken glass of shops that had been looted, and the burned-out wrecks of cars, set alight in the riots which erupted in the country after Hani's murder. As Mandela recalls in his autobiography:

> The country was fragile. There were concerns that Hani's death might trigger a racial war, with the youth deciding that their hero should become a martyr for whom they would lay down their own lives (1994: 599).

Had it not been for Mandela's eminently sane and generous intervention (ibid.: 600), South Africa's peaceful transition to majority rule might never have happened.

A hero of the liberation struggle, lionised by the country's black youth, as Mandela acknowledges, Hani had returned to South Africa when the Communist Party was unbanned in 1990 and had been elected General Secretary of the SACP in 1991. In 1962, he had joined Umkhonto we Sizwe (The Spear of the Nation), the armed wing of the ANC, and was eventually its Chief of Staff (1987-1992), until the armed struggle was officially suspended. Repeatedly detained, tried and sentenced under the Suppression of Communism Act, he was regarded as one of the deadliest enemies of the *apartheid* regime. At least two previous attempts on his life had been made whilst he was in exile in Lesotho in the 1980s.

Educated at a Roman Catholic primary school, where he developed an especial interest in Latin, which was then still used for all services, he matriculated at Lovedale in 1958, the year in which the first edition of *Acta Classica* was published.

While at Lovedale, he joined the ANC Youth League (1957) and, after matriculating, went to the University of Fort Hare to read Latin and English (1959-1961).[9] At Fort Hare, he became involved in the protests against the transfer of the university to the Department of Bantu Education (1959; see Chapter 1) and was suspended for his contribution to the campaign against the declaration of the Republic of South Africa. Consequently, he went to Rhodes University from where he graduated with a BA in Latin and English in 1962. According to Gastrow (1992: 92), the fact that a number of Hani's teachers lost their jobs in 1954 for protesting against the introduction of Bantu Education (see Chapter 1), played a formative role in the development of his politics.

In a brief autobiography ('My Life'), published on the ANC's official website,[10] Hani states that the introduction of Bantu Education which 'was designed to indoctrinate Black pupils to accept and recognise the supremacy of the white man over the blacks in all spheres', paved the way for his involvement in the struggle. It was furthermore at Fort Hare, which he describes as a 'liberal campus' (in 1959), that he was exposed to Marxist ideas 'and the scope and nature of the racist capitalist system'.

Immediately after stating that his 'conversion to Marxism' also deepened his 'non-racial perspective', Hani writes:

My early Catholicism led to my fascination with Latin studies and English literature. These studies in these two courses were gobbled up by me and I became an ardent lover of English, Latin and Greek literature, both modern and classical. My studies of literature further strengthened my hatred of all forms of oppression, persecution and obscurantism. The action of tyrants as portrayed in various literary works also made me hate tyranny and institutionalised oppression.

Immediately after this paragraph, Hani notes that he joined the underground South African Communist Party in 1961 – the year South Africa became a republic – as he realised that 'national liberation, though essential, would not bring about economic liberation'.

Hani clearly believed that there was no cleavage between literature, politics and economics. The fact that he appropriated classical and other literatures to such an extent that they became integral to his identity and his political struggle against oppression and tyranny reveals that here at least was one isiXhosa-speaker who had made the connections both Wakerley and Els deem improbable a generation later.

Classical literature and struggle identities

Another more famous *alumnus* of Fort Hare, some twenty years before Hani, was, of course, Nelson Mandela, whose performance, while in prison on Robben Island, as Creon in Sophocles' *Antigone* has been the subject of much discussion in analyses of the reception of classical Greek drama as struggle or protest theatre in colonial contexts, and thereafter as theatre which appropriates and fashions new versions of the classical canon in the postcolony.

It should also be noted that this incident, referred to in Mandela's autobiography *Long Walk to Freedom*, has been shamelessly exploited by Departments of Classics in South African universities (including my own), in an effort to attract black students to the discipline, perceived frequently by black students as the last outpost of white intellectual indulgence and cultural narcissism.

What Mandela actually said about the *Antigone* is worth repeating. One Christmas, probably in the late 1960s, the prisoners' amateur dramatic society chose the famous Greek tragedy as its annual production. At Fort Hare, Mandela had played the role of John Wilkes Booth (the assassin of Abraham Lincoln) and in prison he recalls the 'modest revival' of his 'thespian career':

> I performed in only a few dramas, but I had one memorable role: that of Creon, the king of Thebes, in Sophocles' *Antigone*. I had read some of the classic Greek plays in prison, and found them enormously elevating. What I took out of them was that character was measured by facing up to difficult situations and that a hero was a man who would not break down even under the most trying circumstances (1994: 441).

Volunteering his services for the play, Mandela was *asked* to play the role of Creon and, some twenty-five years later, it is significant what he remembers from the play: the wisdom of Creon in the early speeches 'when he suggests that experience is the foundation of leadership and that obligations to the people take precedence over loyalty to an individual' (ibid.: 441). Mandela, presumably quoting from memory as no precise reference is given, recalls the following lines from Creon's first speech:

> There's no other way to test a man,
> To learn the true temper of his heart and mind,
> Than by seeing him practise the use of power.
> My own opinion is that any king
> Whose rule is absolute, who locks his lips
> From fear, and refuses to seek advice, is doomed
> And dangerous. And next to him, I hate
> A man who sets his friends above the state
> > *Antigone* 176-183; tr. McLeish

These lines Mandela remembers in the following truncated synopsis:

> Of course you cannot know a man completely, his character, his principles, sense of judgment, not till he's shown his colours, ruling the people, making laws. Experience, there's the test (ibid.: 441).

On the negative side, Mandela then refers to Creon's merciless treatment of his enemies and his refusal to listen to anyone 'but his own inner demons', before concluding:

> His inflexibility and blindness ill become a leader, for a leader must temper justice with mercy. It was Antigone who symbolized our struggle; she was, in her own way, a freedom fighter, for she defied the law on the ground that it was unjust (ibid.: 442).

Mandela's somewhat selective recall of the 'wisdom' of Creon relates directly to a fundamental principle of the African National Congress, recently demonstrated in the ousting of the former leader (and president) Thabo Mbeki (2008) and the election of Jacob Zuma (2009): that the collective is more important than the individual. This belief was not only essential to the politics of classical Athens, but is also an important ethical principle in all southern African black communities, crystallised in the expression 'a person is a person through other persons' (Lambert 2000: 41-55). In contemporary South African politics, the ANC has struggled with the personality cult which has developed around certain leaders (e.g. Mandela himself, and Zuma) and has exposed weaknesses in the traditional African belief, over-romanticised by white missionary ethnographers. Perhaps the ambiguity of 'obligations to the people take precedence over loyalty to an individual' and 'ruling the people, making laws' in Mandela's account of Creon's speech is suggestive of this tension between the demands of the collective and the responsibilities of the leader. That 'a leader must temper justice with mercy' and be a good listener seems to me to be a fitting comment on Mandela's presidency. However, what is especially striking about his brief comment on Sophocles' *Antigone* is his identification with Antigone as the freedom fighter, precisely because she 'defied the law on the ground that it was unjust'. That a man like Mandela, from a rigidly patriarchal African tradition, who escaped an arranged marriage, can so readily identify with the *female* heroine of an ancient Greek tragedy seems to me to be an especially interesting example of the malleability of gender identification, subject to an overriding political ideology which privileges the collective at the expense of the individual: notably, Mandela refers not to 'my struggle', but '*our* struggle'. Thus Hani and Mandela exemplify the ways in which classical texts can be appropriated by the oppressed and thus become 'resistant discourses', in which the identities of the 'communist' and the 'freedom fighter' are located – especially striking in South Africa where the study of the Classics has been so implicit in the ideologies of the ruling élites (see Chapters 1 and 2).

That white South African poets, playwrights, theatre practitioners and academics have appropriated classical texts as contributions to the struggle against *apartheid* has been well documented and has become almost a stock theme in Reception Studies (e.g. Hardwick 2007: 49-51). However, extravagant claims about the significance of these performances of classical drama to the struggle – for example, the suggestion that Euripides' *Medea* was 'a crucial text in the war against South African *apartheid*' (Hall 2004: 25) – are nonsense.

Hall's claim is based on an article published by Betine van Zyl Smit in *Akroterion* in 1992. A graduate of the University of Stellenbosch, where she completed her doctorate on dramatic versions of the Medea myth, van Zyl Smit, then lecturing at the University of the Western Cape, one of the universities established for 'coloureds' during the *apartheid* era, is rather more guarded in her claims. In the process of bringing Guy Butler's play *Demea* to the attention of South African classicists, van Zyl Smit notes that Butler 'wrote this drama more than 30 years ago', but 'political circumstances in South Africa made it impossible for the play to be staged until 1990' when the play was published (1992: 73). Butler, a professor of English at Rhodes University in Grahamstown, states that his play was explicitly based on Euripides' *Medea*:

> I was particularly struck by the *Medea* of Euripides, which dealt with an issue much on my mind: racial and cultural prejudice ... In writing *Demea*, I have turned the *Medea* into a political allegory of the South African situation as I saw it, at the height of the idealistic Verwoerdian mania (ibid.: 75).

Butler clarifies this in a letter to the author:

> My only source was a translation of Euripides – and, of course, South African history just prior to the Great Trek for the setting, and Verwoerdian ethnic philosophy for much of the debate (ibid.: n. 2).

Although van Zyl Smit offers a valiant defence of this horribly contrived play, which features Demea, a black Tembu princess, Captain Jonas Barker (the Jason figure), a British officer, who ends up leading a mixed-race 'trek', Kroon (Creon), the leader of a whites-only 'trek', and Jonas' betrayal of Demea for Kroon's daughter and the whites-only party, the play has not been well received by critics. Van Zyl Smit notes this in reference to the 1990 production which 'was met by a critically hostile response from the left' and then cites the reviews of two white male critics, both of whom seem eminently sane.

Willoughby, for instance, notes that 'this meandering rewrite of Euripides' *Medea* is dull, endless and desperately shallow – a veritable proof of the deadness of a certain brand of starry-eyed liberalism in the 'new' South Africa'. De Kock comments on Butler's 'vastly dated and simplified view of the Great SA Race Problem' (ibid.: 80). One presumes that it is this critique of Butler's old-fashioned white liberalism which earns van Zyl Smit's disapproval ('from the left'). Van Zyl Smit's conclusion is typical of the 'inclusive' political discourse of the early 1990s, after the liberation of Mandela and the 'unbanning' of the ANC and other organizations, and during the constitutional negotiations (see Chapter 1):

> The political theme of the drama, that the betrayal of trust between black and white will inevitably lead to catastrophe and that co-operation between the races is the only way ahead, is of paramount importance in the South Africa of the 1990s (ibid.: 80).

Laudable as this is, it does not make Butler's version of *Medea* a 'crucial text in the war against *apartheid*'. On the contrary, Els objected to including this text in the Classics curriculum at Fort Hare:

> We do not (yet) have a *Demea*, not by a Guy Butler from a Western background, but by a Black South African author from an African background (1994: 166).

Objections of this kind could also be raised against the many productions of Greek tragedies during the *apartheid* years – not the early 1990s when most *apartheid* legislation had been repealed or was in the process of being repealed. I recall, during the particularly repressive

116

1980s, productions of *Antigone* or Aeschylus' *Libation Bearers*, produced by white English-speaking directors and largely for white English-speaking audiences on 'liberal' university campuses, which were designed to comment on acts of political violence and gross injustice, but ended up 'preaching to the converted' and simply confirmed 'struggle' or oppositional identities. Rather than being 'crucial texts in the war against *apartheid*' such productions often seemed to have the reverse effect: by universalising the problem (e.g. the conflict between individual conscience and state repression) and underlining the antiquity of its occurrence, these productions, in my experience, frequently engendered a resigned passivity and blunted the urgency needed for political struggle, certainly among the white 'liberal' community. Rather than challenging an audience to examine its conscience, productions of this kind seemed simply to reinforce the very European nature of that conscience. This contrasts markedly with the experiences of Hani and Mandela, who seem to have internalised and appropriated classical texts as integral features of their 'struggle' identities – as *African* sites of resistance against *apartheid*.

Rather different are the very few versions of Greek theatre which originate in the black communities (e.g. Hardwick 2007: 49) or include black performers and indigenous dances and languages as an integral part of the 'workshop' process, for example, the Fleishman-Reznek collaborations in the post-*apartheid* period (van Zyl Smit 2007: 80-2; Steinmeyer 2007: 152-73), or those which weave black struggle or exile narratives into versions of Greek tragedy (e.g. Hammerschlag's *Suppliants*). However, these too suffer from the fact that they are usually directed by white directors in university drama departments and are aimed at white middle class audiences, often at expensive Arts Festivals, where the audience is generally attuned to the cleverness of the intertextuality. Whether versions of Greek tragedy are more 'authentically African' simply because they contain black performers, African languages (e.g. isiXhosa in Farber's 2003 version of the Electra myth) and dance, and extracts from the hearings and findings of the Truth and Reconciliation Commission, is debatable. In the South African context, what is African authenticity and who decides this? Who is an African?

When Thabo Mbeki made his well-known 'I am an African' speech in 1996, when the new South African constitution was adopted, he situated himself in a tradition of identity discourses reaching back to

Léopold Senghor's concept of 'négritude' and 1960s Black Consciousness. However, what is startlingly innovative, in Gevisser's opinion (2007: 326), is the way in which Mbeki fashions an inclusive Africanness which includes Afrikaner, Indian and Chinese 'migrants':

> While classic Africanness, from Garvey to Biko, fashions a black African identity outside of and in opposition to white European hegemony, Mbeki achieves the supreme act of self-definition: he appropriates and assimilates the identity of his oppressor and uses it to define himself: 'Being a part of all these people, and in the knowledge that none dare contest the assertion, I shall claim that I am an African!' (ibid.: 326).

However, as Chipkin has argued in his analysis of this speech (2007: 101-2), this assimilation of the identity of the oppressor, which suggests a generous inclusiveness, results in the construction of an African identity, which actually excludes those oppressors who have not at the very least acknowledged the injustices of the past. In other words, Mbeki's constantly shifting definition of African identity 'situates "being African" in the context of the struggle against colonialism' (ibid.: 102). Furthermore, his movement between 'being African' and 'being South African' seems to generate the kind of ambiguous identity formerly shaped by British colonialism. Perhaps it is no surprise to learn that Mbeki studied Latin at Lovedale (Gevisser 2007: 94).

In the light of Mbeki's difficulty in articulating what he means by 'being African', one should be especially careful in assigning 'African authenticity' to postcolonial appropriations of Greek tragedy which, in their dramatic negotiation between past and present, often generate the kinds of ambiguity suggested by Mbeki's speech. Rather than being 'authentically African', appropriations of the classical tradition, these versions of Greek tragedy often have more to say about the construction of white middle-class South African identities.

Mbeki's speeches, often replete with references to Shakespeare, Victorian literature and the Bible, reveal the influence of the kind of literary and religious education nurtured at Lovedale and the identity issues this raises. Similarly, John Tengo Jabavu at Lovedale in the late nineteenth century and his son at Fort Hare in the first half of the twentieth century also raise important questions about the appropriation of the classical tradition and black identity. Because of Jabavu Senior's initial support for the infamous Natives Land Act of 1913, he was severely criticised by many black leaders as a pro-white, pro-Boer 'sell-out';[11] subsequently, his son attempted to defend his father's 'one great mistake' (ibid.: 91-3). At a Christian convention in the USA in 1931, D.D.T. Jabavu referred to his identity and its relationship with missionary education in the following striking ways: 'I stand here not as a type of the Africans in my country, because I am really an accident thrown up on top of those multitudes who are standing in the background' (in Higgs 1997: 69) and 'Every black man who is a leader of any importance is a product of missionary work. Outside of missionary work there is no leadership' (ibid.).

Here Jabavu, the first black South African to graduate from London University and the first professor of Latin at Fort Hare, reveals his acute awareness that he belongs to a European-educated élite with enormous social and educational responsibilities. Attempting to reconcile his European education with his African identity, which the political system constantly reinforced, Jabavu's words 'because I am really an accident thrown up on top' suggest his discomfort with an identity imposed on him by his education. Furthermore the words 'a product of missionary work' evoke an artificially manufactured subjectivity. Despite his intense political involvement, especially in the campaign against the Hertzog Bills (see Chapter 2), which succeeded in disenfranchising African voters in the Cape (Higgs 1997: 93, 103, 114), Jabavu, because of his support for the Non-European Unity Movement in the 1940s, was labelled by the more radical Africanists (in the ANC Youth League) as an old-fashioned 'African liberal' (ibid.: 137),[12] who was clearly uncomfortable with the politics of boycotts and protests (ibid. 142). Despite his perceived liberalism, Jabavu did not join the non-racial Liberal party when it was formed in 1953 (ibid.: 156). Both Jabavus illustrate what Fanon explores in *Black Skin, White Masks* (1967): how does a black person disinter his/her identity from the European discourses into which his colonial education, especially in the classics, has inserted him? To recall one of Fanon's famous passages:

The black schoolboy in the Antilles, who in his lessons is forever talking about 'our ancestors, the Gauls', identifies himself with the explorer, the bringer of civilization, the white man who carries

119

truth to savages – an all-white truth. There is identification – that
is, the young Negro subjectively adopts a white man's attitude
(1967: 147).

Similarly, the black South African schoolboy at Lovedale or Zonnebloem
or Mariannhill in the colonial period, although there may be some
difference in the ways in which Protestantism and Catholicism affected
black identities. Intellectuals such as the Jabavus and Grendon
strongly identified with the 'bringer of civilization' and the carrier of
'truth', but both were bitterly disillusioned when they discovered that
the civilization they so admired was a glittering veneer. When Italy
invaded Abyssinia in 1935, D.D.T. Jabavu wrote:

> ... After hearing a great deal for twenty years about the rights of
> small nations, self-determination, Christian ideals, the inviolabil-
> ity of treaties, humane warfare, the sacredness of one's plighted
> word, the glory of European civilization, and so forth, the brief
> history of the last eight months have scratched this European
> veneer and revealed the White savage hidden beneath (quoted in
> Higgs 1997: 125).

In the very pages of the newspaper founded by his father, Jabavu
deliberately subverts the discourse of civilization and savagery and
hurls it back at his colonial masters. Having internalised the voices of
civilization in the course of his education, he seems to loathe that part
of himself which has been colonised: hence perhaps his use of the
dung-heap metaphor discussed above. In more recent times, Nobel
Peace Prize winner, Archbishop Desmond Tutu, also the product of a
missionary education, reflected similarly on his identity:

> I internalised what others had decided was to be my identity ...
> And when I looked inside me and saw this man-made caricature I
> bridled with anger and hatred and contempt of this false self. I
> then projected it outwards to those who outwardly looked like me.
> Before my superior white overlords I quaked with demeaning
> obsequiousness and before those who looked like the thing I hated
> and despised I was harsh and abrasive (2006: 10).

In the process of recognizing the creation of this 'false self', Tutu liberates himself from it without resorting to the kind of *othering* (this time of European civilization) which manufactured the identity he came to loathe. What perhaps distinguishes the Jabavus and Grendon from Hani and Mandela is that the latter use classical literature *strategically* as part of a wider political identity, accepting that which resonates with their fight against oppression, but refusing to allow their European-style education to make 'man-made caricatures' of them, trapped in a liminal zone between the polarities of 'savagery' and 'civilization', rural and urban, as constructed for them.[13]

Vilakazi, Mariannhill and black identity

Focussing exclusively on classical literature and black identities ignores related identity struggles in the field of Zulu literature. Benedict Vilakazi (1906-1947), the father of Zulu literature and the first black academic to be appointed to the staff of an all-white South African university in 1935, where he was capped by Hofmeyr in his role as Chancellor (Paton 1964: 240), was involved in a famous literary dispute in the late 1930s with his contemporary, Herbert Dhlomo, another iconic figure in the history of Zulu letters.[14]

Ostensibly about the use of rhyme in Zulu poetry, this dispute, as Attwell has argued, revealed the dilemma confronting the nationalist black intellectual of the period: to modernise traditional Zulu literature by using Western poetic forms and metres (Vilakazi's position), or to 'traditionalise modernity' by stamping 'modern literary self-conscious-ness with the stamp of Africanity' (Dhlomo's position) (Attwell 2005: 77-110).

Reflecting on his poetics shortly before his death, Vilakazi recalled his education at the monastery of Mariannhill, which included the study of Latin and inevitable exposure to the rhythm of the monastic day and the ringing of the bell to mark the *Angelus*:

... as a college boy I was attracted by a very big church bell called 'Angelus' which rang with its mellow tone wafted over forests and mountains. I do not know why it became a habit that at 9 every Sunday we would listen to its voice with unsatisfied delight, for we could not express our feelings, until one day in a Latin class our

121

lecturer who gloried in Classics, noticed the ringing of this bell. The sound threw him into ecstasy and he said it brought back to him his home in Germany, where, in the city cathedral, there hung a bell with this inscription: 'Vivos voco, mortuous plango, fulgura frango'. My understanding of these lines brought me perpetual content, ever afterwards whenever I heard the toll of this Angelus. The quotation was at once connected in my mind with the old *Ngibengiyazibize, ziyasabela* [a phrase from an orally performed Zulu praise poem]. To my mind both these lines are great poetry. When I read them my mind is filled with pleasant recognition. I can hear the echoing broken cliffs, visualise thick forests and winding rivers. While on the other hand on hearing the tolling of the 'Angelus' for a funeral, or, on the approaching of the storm with heavy dark clouds, a feeling of safety and relief from fear is immediately engendered by the remembrance of the 'Angelus' tolling on a Sunday morning and the people streaming to church along different winding paths, up and down the echoing mountains. The swinging of the bell is felt in the rhythm of the Latin composition, while the Zulu line presents a queer scanning, imitating the wafted waves of a re-echoing voice: *donga zeLangwe, Ngibengiyazibize, ziyesabela* [the echoing of the precipitous battle fields of Langwe] (in Attwell 2005: 88).

Apart from the fact that the recall of a line from an orally transmitted Zulu praise poem and the memory of a Latin inscription on a German cathedral bell, together with the sensuousness of their rhythms, suggest the scope of Vilakazi's aesthetics (the traditional and its relationship to modernity), it is noteworthy that his memory of the inscription is situated in a Latin class taught by a teacher 'who gloried in Classics'. A German-educated Roman Catholic priest thus contributes to Vilakazi's poetic attempts to reconcile his African identity with his very European mission education. The tolling of the 'Angelus', remembered by Vilakazi as the name of the bell itself, is especially interesting.

As Green has suggested in his semi-historical novel on the foundation of Mariannhill and its daughter houses in South Africa (2008), the Cistercian custom of ringing bells to mark the hours of the sacred office was frequently interpreted by non-Christian people (e.g. the Turks in Bosnia and the Zulus in Natal) as a form of offensive aural colonialism which threatened the power of the local pasha or chieftain. That Vilakazi remembers the sound with delight reveals the extent to which he has internalised the European features of his socialization: that this delight should be 'unsatisfied', 'for we could not express our feelings' suggests the tensions engendered by the situation itself – a black schoolboy in a monastery classroom with an authoritarian white priest who is permitted to express his 'ecstasy' in front of his captive class, one of whom has to postpone his delight for the future pleasure of memory. As Vilakazi chooses to remember the incident, the power dynamics in the classroom do not result in the use of Latin to intimidate the young schoolboy: on the contrary, his conscious equation of the Latin motto with the line from Zulu traditional poetry suggests an easy movement between Western and African literatures, which does not valorize one at the expense of the other. In negotiating his identity as an African writer, Vilakazi reveals how he has appropriated his classical education and made it an essential feature of his identity as a Zulu poet.[15]

The role of the Classics in the identity discourses of mission-educated Black intellectuals in the late nineteenth and early twentieth centuries seems very far removed from the thought-worlds of the black students at Unitra and the University of Fort Hare discussed at the beginning of this chapter. The destruction of the mission school system by the behemoth of Bantu Education obviously resulted in the conviction that education and vocational training are synonymous; the agonistic relationship between the two and its close links to the forging of black nationalist identities has been effectively smothered by the remorselessness of *apartheid* and the crass antithetical thinking which underpinned it, inherited as we have seen from the British imperialist period. That European canonical literature, specifically English literature, can be used as a feature of struggle identities or 'resistant discourses' occasionally surfaces in the speeches of mission-educated politicians (such as Thabo Mbeki), but the central role of the study of the Classics in the formation of the identities of black intellectuals such as the Jabavus, Grendon and Vilakazi is now appreciated, ironically, not by South African classicists, who should be eager to reclaim the study of the Classics from its racist past and invest it in an African future, but by scholars in English Studies (such as de Kock, Christison and Woeber).

Conclusion

Opening these three windows on to the reception of the Classics in South Africa has revealed how inextricably intertwined the study of the civilizations of Greece and Rome has been with the political and cultural history of colonialism (both Dutch and British) and nationalisms (Afrikaner and African). Furthermore, crucial stages in the forging of important South African identities have been marked by an engagement with the classical tradition at periods when this tradition was considered essential for educational, social and political advancement. The links between the classical tradition and powerful elites suggest how deeply embedded the teaching of the Classics has been in the unequal power relations which characterize race relations in South Africa's history. However, this does not mean that the teaching of the Classics should be abandoned along with other colonialist baggage. What is the situation in South Africa at present?

In post-colonial South Africa, the study of the Classics is confined to a few universities, where courses in Greek and Latin attract a mere handful of students and courses in Classical Civilization, especially Classical Mythology, feature as electives within Arts and Social Science degrees. The study of Classical Greek has disappeared from the schools; Latin has almost vanished as well. In 2008, a mere twenty-two students in the entire country sat the Matriculation examination in Latin. No school offers Classical Civilization as a subject.

In the universities where Greek and Latin are offered, the languages are under constant attack from penny-pinching Deans or rather, Line Managers, many of whom have turned their backs on education for the worship of Performance Management Systems or PMS, which has imported the politics of the factory floor (and the stress with which the acronym is conventionally associated) into the classroom. In such a context, where an instrumentalist barbarism prevails, debate about the future of the Humanities in the South African context has become linked, inevitably, to the fate of Departments of Classics. In my own university, where the Classics have been taught and researched for a century, a recent attack on the Department generated intense debate about the purpose of the traditional Humanities in a multi-cultural university in South Africa with the kind of 'skills agenda' which reflects the shift in Humanities teaching in the 'contemporary knowledge society' (van der Hoven 2003: 85-96). Exploring this through literature (a technique I used for reflections on identity in the Introduction) can clarify the contours of the debate.

In *Elizabeth Costello*, J.M. Coetzee offers, as one of eight 'lessons', a provocative reflection on the role of the Humanities in Africa. Costello, a fictional Australian novelist, visits South Africa in order to attend the graduation of her sister (Blanche), a former classicist turned Catholic nun (Sister Bridget), who became a medical missionary and is now the administrator of the Hospital of the Blessed Mary at Marianhill in KwaZulu.[1]

For her work in 'rural Zululand', Sister Bridget receives an honorary doctorate from a university in Johannesburg and, as is customary, delivers the graduation address to the assembled graduands in the Faculty of Humanities. In the course of this address, Sister Bridget links the origins of textual scholarship in the *studia humanitatis* in Western universities with the need to interpret the Bible as accurately as possible, in the wake of the classical Greek texts which were redis-covered by the West after the fall of Constantinople:

> The linguistic command that was intended to be applied to the Greek New Testament could be perfected only by immersing one-self in these seductive pre-Christian texts. In no time, as one might expect, the study of these texts, later to be called the classics, had become an end in itself (2003: 121).

Sister Bridget goes on to argue, in what she deems her 'brief and crude account' of the origins of the humanities, that the study of the classics (the *literae humaniores*) at first was not an end in itself, but a means to understanding the 'meaning of redemption'. Biblical scholar-ship and studies in 'Greek and Roman antiquity' were yoked precisely in order to clarify how the redeemed state differed from the unre-deemed, that is, mankind in his fallen state (Greece and Rome) before the incarnation of Christ. Finally, Sister Bridget, reflecting on the meaninglessness of modern *studia humanitatis*, diverted as they are 'from their proper goal', concludes:

> The *studia humanitatis* have taken a long time to die, but now, at the end of the second millennium of our era, they are truly on their deathbed. All the more bitter should be that death, I would say, since it has been brought about by the monster enthroned by those studies as first and animating principle of the universe: the monster of reason, mechanical reason (ibid.: 123).

In the ensuing conversations between Sister Bridget, Elizabeth Costello and members of the Humanities Faculty at the graduation lunch and later at Marianhill, which Elizabeth visits, Coetzee probes further the implications of Sister Bridget's views on the death of the humanities and the classical tradition. Arguing that Hellenism was the only vision of the 'good life' which humanism was able to offer as an alternative to Christianity, Sister Bridget reminds her sister that 'when Hellenism failed – which was inevitable, since it had nothing whatever to do with the lives of real people – humanism went bankrupt' (2003: 132). At Marianhill, where the novelist is confronted with the lives of real people in Africa, including that of the mission's sculptor (Joseph), who has produced endless carvings of Christ suffering on the cross, she asks of her sister:

> What are you doing, importing into Africa, importing into Zululand, for God's sake, this utterly alien *Gothic* obsession with the ugliness and mortality of the human body? If you have to import Europe into Africa, is there not a better case for importing the Greeks? (ibid.: 139-40).

Sister Bridget's answer, which recalls the comparative studies of Bryant and others referred to in Chapter 2, is most pertinent to this study:

> Are you aware that when Europeans first came into contact with the Zulus, educated Europeans, men from England with public school educations behind them, they thought they had rediscovered the Greeks? They said so quite explicitly. They took out their sketch blocks and drew sketches in which Zulu warriors with

their spears and their clubs and their shields are shown in exactly the same attitudes, with exactly the same physical proportions, as the Hectors and Achilles we see in nineteenth century illustrations of the *Iliad*, except that their skins are dusky ... Sparta in Africa; that is what they thought they had found. For decades those same ex-public schoolboys, with their romantic idea of Greek antiquity, administered Zululand on behalf of the Crown. They *wanted* Zululand to be Sparta. They *wanted* the Zulus to be Greeks. So to Joseph and his father and his grandfather the Greeks are not a remote foreign tribe at all. They were offered the Greeks, by their new rulers, as a model of the kind of people they ought to be and could be. They were offered the Greeks and they rejected them. Instead, they looked elsewhere in the Mediterranean world. They chose to be Christians, followers of the living Christ. Joseph has *chosen* Jesus as his model. Speak to him. He will tell you (ibid.: 140).

In contrast to the Oxbridge-educated colonialists who offered their 'barbarian subjects' the false ideals of a romanticized Hellenism, Sister Bridget claims that she (and the Church), rooted in the realities of African suffering, promise nothing but help to make this suffering bearable. Later, as Elizabeth Costello is about to return to Australia, her debate with her sister re-surfaces and Sister Bridget reminds her that she has backed a 'loser':

If you had put your money on a different Greek you might still have stood a chance. Orpheus instead of Apollo. The ecstatic instead of the rational. Someone who changes form, changes colour, according to his surroundings. Someone who can die but then come back. A chameleon. A phoenix. Someone who appeals to women. Because it is women who live closest to the ground. Someone who moves among the people, whom they can touch – put their hand into the side of, feel the wound, smell the blood. But you didn't, and you lost. You went for the wrong Greeks, Elizabeth (ibid.: 145).

A month after her return to Australia, the novelist reflects on her reunion with her sister in the form of a 'letter' about their mother and her friendship with a retired lawyer in an old-age home, one of whose hobbies was painting in watercolours.[2] Their mother had 'sat' for the reclusive painter, who was disfigured by a laryngectomy; so, subsequently, did Elizabeth Costello herself, who spontaneously posed bare-breasted for him. Attempting to make sense of this act and her sojourn in Africa, Costello returns to the debate about the Greeks and the Hellenistic aesthetic:

> Where did I learn that pose, gazing calmly into the distance with my robe hanging about my waist like a cloud and my divine body on show? *From the Greeks*, I now realize, Blanche: from the Greeks and from what generations of Renaissance painters made of the Greeks (ibid.: 149).

Noting that their discussion about humanism and the humanities avoided talk about 'humanity', which she believes she revealed when uncovering her breasts for the watercolourist, Costello concludes the story of her 'letter':

> The humanities teach us humanity. After the centuries-long Christian night, the humanities give us back our beauty, our human beauty. That was what you forgot to say. That is what the Greeks teach us, Blanche, the right Greeks. Think about it (ibid.: 151).

In the current academic environment in South African universities, in which, as I mentioned above, a crude managerialism prevails, focused more and more on research for research's sake, preferably in subsidy-earning publications in a designated set of journals, Sister Bridget's arguments have especial relevance. The study of the humanities has been so 'instrumentalized' that the study of a discipline for its own sake, for the rare pleasure of even a 'mechanical' *explication de texte*, is rarely encountered. In the teaching of foreign languages, for instance, courses such as 'Commercial German' or 'Business French' or 'English for Commerce Students' or 'Communicative isiZulu' have ensured that most of our language graduates can find their way around a European or South African supermarket, but have probably never heard of Corneille or Racine, Goethe or Schiller, Blake or Austen,

Vilakazi or Dhlomo. Sister Bridget's argument that the uncoupling of the study of texts from their 'proper goal' has ushered in the death throes of the Humanities in South Africa is not without some merit. However, it is precisely the re-coupling of the study of the Humanities to 'goals' such as business, sport and travel, arguably forms of secular religion, which, in my opinion, will result in the death of the tradition-ally-conceived *studia humanitatis*.

Elizabeth Costello's arguments are not especially convincing. Sister Bridget first mentions Winckelmann at the graduation lunch, as an example of a humanist and classical scholar who believed that Greece 'provided a better civilizational ideal than Judaeo-Christianity' (2003: 130). It is also evident, in her account of British colonials sketching the Zulus as latter-day Greeks (ibid.: 140), that Winckelmann's homoerotic, idealized reflections on Greek representations of male beauty played an important role in her classical training and in her misconceptions of Hellenism. Costello's thoughts on the 'beauty' which the Humanities give back to us are also suffused with Winckelmann's aesthetics, even though she transfers his gaze to the female body in her 'letter' (ibid.: 149-50). In fact, in attempting to convince her sister that she has backed the 'right' Greeks after all, Costello simply repeats a version of the arguments her sister has already demolished. Coetzee thus suggests that the study of the Humanities in Africa (and especially the study of the Classics) is trapped in an intellectual *cul-de-sac*, between the Scylla of instrumentalism and the Charybdis of a meaningless 'art for beauty's sake'. Doubtless Sister Bridget would approve of courses in Hellenistic Greek at South African universities, which explicitly link the study of the Classics with biblical exegesis, but what would she or her sister make of courses which focus not exclusively on the 'beauty' of the Greeks or Romans, but also on the sheer ugliness and suffering which link Greece and Rome with Africa? The treatment of women, slaves and foreigners, infant exposure, abortion, rape, incest, disease, war, land confiscation, tyranny, mercenaries, political instability, xenophobia, bribery and corruption: Greek city-states and Rome, from Republic to Empire, provide endless examples of all of these (and more), and thus a study of the Classics in this way, removing Winckelmann's deeply sanitized lenses, can provide an acute and perceptive commentary on *our* shared humanity (that is, of Africans and proto-Europeans).

In 1993 Mogomme Masoga and I, in collaboration with colleagues at the Universities of the Western Cape, Zimbabwe and Malawi, embarked on a research exercise aimed at assessing perceived areas of similarity and difference between African societies and classical antiquity (Lambert and Masoga 1994: 75-82). Twelve passages were selected from Roman lyric and elegy, Greek and Roman epic, Greek social history, Greek philosophy, Greek tragedy, Greek medicine, Roman philosophy, Roman history, Greek comedy and Greek mythology. A questionnaire containing the pre-selected passages and questions set on them was issued to a group of students representing languages and cultural groupings in South Africa, Zimbabwe, Malawi and Namibia. An analysis of the responses revealed that this group of African students reacted with most interest to the following areas (in order of preference): Greek and Roman rituals, the relationship between myth and ritual, the oral tradition as revealed in Homeric epic, and social and political problems, which had especial resonance in their respective African contexts.

Problems such as the position of women in African society were raised by the passage from Plato's *Republic*; the acute problem of land and re-distribution in Zimbabwe and South Africa was explored through the politics of Tiberius Gracchus; familiar conflicts between traditional, religious beliefs and secular authority were brought to the fore by the extract from Sophocles' *Antigone*; the pressing issues of unemployment and exploitation, as well as the tension often engendered between theory and practice (the academic and the activist?), became the focus of response to Seneca's views on slavery (ibid.: 81).

However, it also became apparent that the students objected to patronising, value-laden comparisons of the following kind: 'they (African cultures) are like us (Greeks and Romans!) in some respects; therefore African culture must have some sort of worth' (ibid.: 82). Furthermore, some respondents objected to comparisons which implied that Africans were 'backward' or trapped in an earlier evolutionary stage and thus appropriate material for comparisons with earlier European civilizations. Perhaps because of the issues raised by the passages chosen for comment, none of the students seemed to accept the notion of 'classical' antiquity: that the civilizations of Greece and Rome were in many ways perfect or ideal or worthy of emulation.

Although the questionnaire for this study tended to manipulate the students into the kinds of responses the compilers wanted to find, the study did suggest that looking at classical antiquity via an African lens can dissolve the binaries European/African (or even Eurocentric/Africanist) which have bedevilled the study of the Classics in South Africa. In this sense, the study of the Classics can be both instrumentalist (as Sister Bridget argued), and can 'teach us humanity', as Elizabeth Costello suggested. The 'right' Greeks, at this moment in South Africa's history, seem to me to be neither of the options Coetzee offers us, but both. If we opt for the 'wrong' Greeks and the study of the Classics remains mired in the various -isms (e.g. colonialism and nationalism) attendant upon the history of the reception and transmission of the discipline in this country, then the discipline will continue to be the preserve of a 'white enclave' and the *studia humanitatis*, in particular the study of the Classics, will be truly on their deathbed.

Notes

Introduction

1. By 'Black', Whitaker clearly means 'of African descent'. The fact that he uses capital letters for 'Black' and 'White' suggests this. However, any use of 'Black' and 'White' in the South African context is loaded with historical and political baggage. South Africans of Indian descent or of mixed race ('Coloureds') could consider themselves 'Black' for political reasons, thus identifying themselves with the struggle against White oppression. White South Africans, for example, of Dutch or British descent, could consider themselves 'African', if they identified with any of the prevailing nationalist discourses attempting to forge an African or specifically South African identity. By 'black students' or 'black classicists', I refer to classicists of colour. See Chipkin's incisive discussion of 'blackness' in the South African political context (2007: 8-9).

2. For theoretical texts which I have found useful, see Ashcroft et al. (1995), Fanon (1986), Said (1995), Woodward (2002), Weedon (2004).

3. For a useful concept of ideology, see Althusser 1984: 36.

4. The black South African author, Sol Plaatje (1876-1932), both protested vigorously against British injustices and identified himself as a loyal British subject as well (Chipkin 2007: 1). See Giliomee and Mbenga 2008: 213.

5. Foucault 1976: 122, 124. For trenchant critiques of Foucault, especially from a feminist perspective, see Bartky (1988), Foxhall (1998), Lloyd (1993), Phelan (1990), Richlin (1998), Sawicki (1994), to name but a few.

6. As Morris's study of the xenophobia experienced by Nigerian and Congolese refugees in Johannesburg illustrates (1999: 75-102). Exiled Zimbabweans have been especially brutally treated; cf. Win 2004: 18.

7. See Chipkin's study (2007) which explores the tensions between 'sameness' and 'difference' in the context of liberal democracy, nationalism and the identity of the South African 'people'.

8. I am aware of the considerable debate surrounding the social, political and ideological 'function' of Greek tragedy and do not mean to suggest that Aeschylus was some sort of poststructuralist *manqué* (see Heath 2006: 253-81 for a very clear outline of this debate). However, as a South African reader of the play at this moment in South Africa's political history, Aeschylus does seem to comment acutely on these themes. For the purposes of this discussion, I have used the OCT of the *Suppliants* edited by Denys Page (1972). Translations are my own.

9. Although, as Vidal-Naquet reminds us (1997: 110), Egypt was not a city-state which could be represented in Argos by a 'proxenos'. Tragedians often created their own political realities.

10. For the Athenians' increasing interest, during the fifth and fourth centuries BCE, in questions of descent, lineage, foreigners and citizens, see Isaac 2004: 109-33, 504. Although Pelasgus and Aeschylus presumably did not understand 'race' in any modern sense, in this exchange, Pelasgus resorts to the kind of racial classification based on ethnic stereotypes, which is disturbingly reminiscent of *apartheid* South Africa.

11. See Vasunia (2001: 33-74) for Aeschylus' portrayal of Egyptians as black, deadly and sexually rapacious as part of tragedy's 'detour through the other', essential to promote Athenian civic ideology. Cf. Vidal-Naquet 1997: 119 and Hall 1989: 162.

12. Descended as they are from the black Epaphos (Aes. *Prom.* 851).

13. Hall (1989: 192-3) convincingly argues that the fifth century Athenian tragedians manipulated the mythical tradition to reflect contemporary political ideology. In 464/463 BCE, the generally accepted date for the first performance of *Suppliants*, selling the democratic process to the Athenian audience and contrasting this with 'barbarian' tyrannies may well have been necessary in the years after the radical reforms of Cleisthenes (cf. Forrest 1960: 232-3). For interpretations which claim that historical events are recalled by the trilogy, see Forrest 1960: 221-41 and Sommerstein 1997: 63-79. For the history of the trilogy's dating problems, see Lloyd-Jones 1990: 262-77 and Conacher 1997: 75-6; for a later dating (461 BCE), see Sommerstein 1997: 77-8. For arguments in favour of an earlier dating, see Scullion 2002: 90-101, who favours dating the play to *c.* 475 BCE: 'In the 470s Themistokles was favouring an anti-Spartan policy, which would naturally entail at least some degree of common cause with Argos; if we must have a suitable historical context, this one seems perfectly plausible. The 'democratic' aspect of Argos in the play is probably no more than the reading of Athenian concerns into the mythical past' (99).

14. Both Danaos and the Danaides use political vocabulary which seems to belong in a democratic polis, not the mythical kingdom of Argos (601, 604 'the sovereign hand of the people', 607). Pelasgus actually uses *'demopraktos'* of the Argive vote (942). Forrest (1960) argues that Aeschylus may well be praising the Argive democracy which accepted the suppliant Themistokles *c.* 470-469 BCE; however, Lloyd-Jones points out (1990: 264-5) that little is known of the Argive constitution in the fifth century and a democratic assembly in mythical Argos is not such an anachronism. Popular assemblies are common in epic kingdoms (see the Homeric epics).

15. *'xenikon astikon'* ('stranger-citizen' 618), which echoes *'astoxenoi'* ('citizen-guests', 356), presumably an Aeschylean invention, which superbly captures the ambiguity of the Danaides' position. On further verbal ambiguities in the play, see Gantz 1978: 279-87.

16. 'Thus rejecting the only role for citizen women sanctioned in ancient Athenian society...' (Hall 1989: 203).

17. Thus possibly looking forward to the next plays in the trilogy (*Egyptians, Danaides*) in which Danaos takes power after the defeat of Argos and the death of Pelasgus. See Winnington-Ingram 1983: 55-72, for a credible reconstruction of the trilogy and satyr play (*Amymone*). Sicherl (1986) and Rösler (1993) argue that *Suppliants* was the second play in the trilogy after the *Egyptians*, in which

the audience was informed of an oracle that Danaos would be killed by a son-in-law, thus motivating his desire to keep his daughters unmarried, and the eventual murders. However, see Hose (2006: 91-8) for trenchant critique of the need for this oracle: as he argues, the use of oracles 'post and ante eventum' are familiar 'narrative techniques' in Greek literature. Hence there are no grounds for arguing that the *Egyptians* was the first play in the trilogy or that the *Suppliants* was either first or second (cf. Conacher 1996: 109-11). There is, after all, only one play extant: what the other plays contained must remain imaginative speculation, despite the tantalizing fragment from the end of the *Danaides*, which certainly convinces Hose that this play was the last in the trilogy (2006: 97 n.6; cf. Podlecki 1975: 5-6).

18. 81-2, 331-2, 335, 337, 392-5, 790, 798-9, 1031-2, 1052-3, 1062-4. Zeitlin (1996: 123-71) suggesting that the trilogy ended with the introduction of the Thesmophoria, believes that the trilogy aimed to 'teach' the Danaides to accept a subordinate feminine role in marriage and celebrate female reproductive power. She argues that the trilogy explores the power struggle between the sexes: persuasion and the tender charm of eros have to triumph over masculine violence, *and* the Danaides' pathological contempt of marriage (cf. MacKinnon 1978: 74-82). Similarly, Zelenak (1998: 45-58) argues that Aeschylus stages a 'gender confrontation' between radical 'femaleness' and 'maleness' to challenge assumptions about marriage and the ideology of gender in the fifth-century Athenian patriarchy.

19. The cries of the Danaides resemble those of the nightingale pursued by the hawk (660-2). Danaos compares his daughters to doves cowering in fear from hawks (223-5). The Danaides are heifers pursued by wolves (351); their Egyptian pursuers are crows with no respect for altars (751), bold dogs (758), wild animals in temper (762-2); the violent herald is a spider (887), a snake and viper (895-6). See Seaford 1987: 111, for animal imagery and the rejection of the marriage theme.

20. 'No other ancient people privileged language to such an extent in defining its own ethnicity' (Hall 1989: 5).

21. Initially commissioned by Border Crossings (1999), the play is available from Sara Stroud, Judy Daish Associates Ltd., 2 St Charles Place, London, W10 6EG.

22. Significantly, 'I have too many languages in my head' is the title of Vigouroux's study of the linguistic practices of African Francophone immigrants in Cape Town (1999: 171-97).

1. The Classics and Afrikaner Identities

1. See the conference booklet compiled and edited by Professor David Wardle of the Classics Department at the University of Cape Town for this information and for the abstracts of the 63 papers delivered (abstracts subsequently published in *Acta Classica* 50, 2007: 171-93, the official journal of CASA).

2. The first Classical Association of South Africa was founded in March 1927, but by 1956 only the Johannesburg Classical Association was still active. CASA as it exists now was established at the first national conference of South African

classicists in Pretoria in April 1956 ('A Report on the Classical Association of South Africa, 1956-1957', *AClass* 1, 1958: 164).

3. Henderson 2004: 90; de Kock, Gonin, La Grange, Lubbe, Pistorius (University of Pretoria)*, Louw, Richards, van Rooy (University of the Orange Free State)*, Smuts (University of Stellenbosch)*, van N Viljoen, von Weber (University of South Africa), Coetzee, Grobler, Potsma, (University of Potchefstroom)*, Paap (University of Cape Town), Lagouros, Naudé (University of the Witwatersrand). The university affiliation is listed as was the case in 1956; many scholars in this list subsequently moved to other South African universities. Asterisks denote Afrikaans-speaking universities at the time.

4. de Kock, Gonin, Lubbe, Naudé, van N Viljoen (Leiden), van Rooy (research at Leiden), Paap, Richards, Smuts (Utrecht).

5. Gonin, Haarhoff (one of the elected Honorary Presidents of CASA), van Rooy (Oxford); van N Viljoen (Cambridge). In contrast, founders of the earlier Classical Association (1927) had all studied at Oxford (Hofmeyr, Edgar, Haarhoff) or Cambridge (Petrie) during their careers, with the exception of Rollo, who was a graduate of Glasgow and Leiden (see Smuts 1960: 18, 20, 26).

6. Henderson 2004: 91 n. 9.

7. In Shell 1994: 79. The Portuguese slaver was captured off the Brazilian coast and, of the 250 children captured, 75 survived the journey to the Cape (Giliomee and Mbenga 2008: 47). The Dutch preferred child slaves at this stage, as they had a better rate of survival than adults (Shell: 79-80). These children were slaves intended for the use of the Dutch East India Company (i.e. public or Company slaves, as opposed to the private slaves of company officials and *burghers*). For van Riebeeck's Latin (and that of his two sons), see van Stekelenburg 2003: 89-90. Abraham van Riebeeck's Latin thesis (Leiden 1673) was apparently the first Latin text by a South African born and bred!

8. Behr (1952: 68) uses the term 'Hottentot', which some now consider offensive (Hilton 2007: 3, n.11). I shall use the preferred 'Khoikhoi', but will retain 'Hottentot' where unavoidable (for example, in White's translation of Hemmy's *oratio*).

9. In contrast with the later Dutch West India Company (WIC), which considered West and Central Africa as its market. Slaves from these areas, who found their way to the Cape, were usually captured from other slavers, in a manner similar to the *Amersfoort* slaves (Shell 1994: 41; for slavery and the WIC, see Parker 2001: 27-9). The slave school was intended for public slaves owned by the Company, but a report by the Scholarch (the board controlling education at the Cape) to the Public Council almost a century later (1779) indicates that almost half the children at the slave school were the slaves of private citizens (Behr 1952: 77-8). This school lasted until 1795 (Shell 1994: 347). Teaching Christianity to slaves, converting and baptizing them raised a number of problems for both the Company and private, slave-owning households. The Synod of Dordrecht (1618) had debated whether children in Christian households, born of 'heathen' slave parents, ought to be baptized and raised as Christians: agreement between the different reformed delegations to the Synod was not reached and the various opinions on pagan baptisms were collected in a document entitled *De Ethnicorum Pueris Baptizandis* (On

whether the children of pagans should be baptized), which was important in the development of the attitudes to slaves in the Dutch colonies. First, it was established that the head of the household (not the Reformed Church or the parents) should decide the religious fate of the slaves, which resulted in as many interpretations as there were households. Secondly, one of the learned opinions in *De Ethnicorum* was that baptized slaves should have the same rights as other Christians and that baptized slaves could not be sold – it was unclear whether this meant not at all, or not to 'heathens' (Shell 1994: 333-4). This opinion raised crucial questions about the nature of slavery itself, the meaning of the 'same rights as Christians', and the marketability of slaves: why baptize slaves at all if they promptly lost their resale value? As Shell remarks: 'In South Africa, slaves were safer investments if they were *not* Christian, a conviction that continued until emancipation' (ibid.: 342). Consequently, Muslim slaves were often preferred (ibid.: 358-62). As far as the Lodge or public slaves were concerned (the Company's 'household'), all children were baptized as Protestant Christians and all baptized slaves were freed at 40 years of age; imported slaves, after 30 years service to the Company (ibid.: 343-4). Cf. Giliomee and Mbenga 2008: 57-8.

10. By 1779 there were slave children in all eight public schools (Behr 1952: 80). At the time of Hemmy's oration (1767) and dissertation (1770), more than half of the VOC's employees at the Cape were Germans (van Stekelenburg 2003: 103). The French Huguenots began arriving at the Cape in 1688, fleeing religious persecution. Sharing the Calvinist version of Christianity with the Dutch settlers, they rapidly acquired the language and mores of the white settler community. Many Afrikaans-speaking families in contemporary South Africa have French Huguenot surnames (Giliomee and Mbenga 2008: 46, 60).

11. Hemmy's *oratio* has been edited and translated by K.D. White, with an introduction by D.H. Varley (1959). References are to this edition. I have used White's translation. Similarly, I have used M.L. Hewett's edition of Hemmy's dissertation (1998), which includes a translation and a useful introduction. Thirty years before Hemmy's public lecture (1737), the freed West African slave, Jacobus Elisa Johannes Capitein, educated at the Latin School at The Hague, delivered his school-leaving *oratio* (*De Vocatione Ethnicorum*), before studying theology at Leiden, where he delivered his dissertation as a lecture in 1742. This dissertation, which seeks to reconcile Christian 'freedom' with slavery, has been edited and translated by G. Parker (2001). A comparative analysis of the works of Hemmy and Capitein would make a fascinating study.

12. White 1959: 10, 13, 21.

13. Published in German in Nuremburg in 1719 and subsequently 'done into English' as *The Present State of the Cape of Good Hope* by a Mr Medley of London, 1731 (Varley's introduction to White's edition, 1959: v n.7). Before Hemmy's account of the Cape, Wilhelm ten Rhyne, a medical doctor in the VOC, had written (in Latin) a *Schediasma de Promontorio Bonae Spei* (Short Account of the Cape of Good Hope, 1686), two-thirds of which was devoted to a negative account of the Hottentots (van Stekelenburg 2003: 91-3).

14. Full title: *Allgemein Historie der Reizen zu Wasser und zu Lände, oder Sammlung aller Reisebeschreibungen* (Leipzig 1744, 21 vols, mostly derived

from the collections of travel histories by Astley and Prévost) (White 1959: 38 n.14).

15. I owe the Tacitean reference to White 1959: 38 n.16. For van Grevenbroek's positive account of the Hottentots, composed in 1695, see van Stekelenburg 2003: 93-102. In contrast to ten Rhyne (n. 13), who spent less than four weeks at the Cape, van Grevenbroek lived in Cape Town and in Stellenbosch for many years (1684-c.1725) and was visited by Kolbe, whose work was clearly influenced by van Grevenbroek's treatise (ibid.: 96).

16. Hemmy's work does not explicitly compare the Hottentots or indigenous peoples with the Greeks or the Romans, in contrast to Lafitau's extraordinary *Moeurs des Sauvages américains aux moeurs des premiers temps* (1724). Haarhoff devotes an entire chapter to the perceived similarities between Stoicism and Calvinist Christianity in his *Vergil in the Experience of South Africa* (1931). Smuts' doctoral thesis at Utrecht was entitled *Die Etiek van Seneca* and Hugo's, also at Utrecht, *Calvyn en Seneca* (*Acta Classica* 2, 1959: 120).

17. For a reliable, general history of South Africa, see, most recently, Giliomee and Mbenga 2008; Davenport 1991 is useful too; for a history of pre-*apartheid* education in South Africa, see Behr and Macmillan 1966; for a still reliable (and once banned) biography of Verwoerd, see Hepple 1967.

18. One should beware of over-emphazising the importance of education in pre-industrial South Africa. Giliomee points out that by as late as 1875, 43 per cent of white children between the ages of five and fifteen were literate (1987: 29). See Giliomee and Mbenga 2008: 95. Faure and his son graduated at Utrecht (Smuts 1960: 8-9, 14).

19. Behr 1952: 160; Behr and Macmillan 1966: 95.

20. Giliomee and Mbenga 2008: 89; Behr 1952: 2.

21. Behr 1952: 182; Behr and Macmillan 1966: 330 (apprenticeships 1834-1838). Emancipation became effective on 1 December 1838 (Giliomee and Mbenga 2008: 91). Lodge slaves had been freed in 1828 (Shell 1994: 403, 418). Shell notes that in 1835 slave records replace the word 'slaves' with 'apprentices' (ibid.: 448)

22. Similarly other Trekker leaders, for example, Retief and Anna Steenkamp, who regarded the equality of liberated slaves with Christian white settlers as against the laws of God (Behr 1952: 46). Paul Kruger claimed that he could prove from the Bible that racial equality was anti-Christian (ibid.: 56). For Trekker racism generally, see Behr 1952: 50-2, 56 (a source biased in favour of the Trekkers). For a full account of the complicated socio-economic and political causes of the Great Trek, see Giliomee and Mbenga 2008: 108-10.

23. Judge's successor was an ordained Scot (the Reverend John Pears) and Faure's A.N.E. Changuion, sent out by Leiden University in 1831 (Smuts 1960: 10-11).

24. A chair of Mathematics already existed (Smuts 1960: 9).

25. For the elementary school curriculum (which excluded Latin), see Behr and Macmillan 1966: 97; for the accessibility of these school to all races, which provoked resentment amongst the Dutch settlers, see Behr 1952: 186; for an example of the curriculum at a black mission school of the period, Behr 1952:

128 (Dutch, Sechuana, arithmetic, reading the Bible); in 1849, Latin and Dutch were on the white school curriculum in Natal (Behr and Macmillan 1966: 112); in 1878 Dutch was not included in the curriculum for state or state-aided primary schools in Natal (ibid.: 116); Behr notes that by the mid-1860s public schools in Natal were open to blacks (ibid.: 334).

26. Sir Langham Dale (Oxford) served as English professor of Classics from 1848 until he was appointed head of education in the Cape Colony in 1859. The Reverend James Cameron (London), Dale's successor, was the first registrar of the University of the Cape of Good Hope when it was established as an examining body in 1873; classicists served on the 1858 Board of Public Examiners and protected the position of Classics, especially Greek in Cape schools; James Gill (Cambridge) succeeded Cameron and Ritchie (Aberdeen, Oxford) Gill (Smuts 1960: 14-16).

27. Professor Basson, a graduate of Stellenbosch and Berlin, and, in the opinion of Smuts writing in 1960, one of South Africa's 'finest classical scholars' also taught in Afrikaans (1960: 29).

28. In particular, the translations of J.P.J. van Rensburg, formerly professor of Greek at Stellenbosch; CASA honoured him for this (Henderson 2007: 103).

29. Nienaber 1974: 2. Other Huguenot descendants at the foundation meeting, apart from the four du Toits present, included the two Malherbes. Of the two Dutch members present, Hoogenhout had emigrated from the Netherlands to South Africa in 1860, Pannevis in 1866. In this respect, Tamarkin comments: 'As in some cases of small "unhistoric" subjugated small nations in Europe, it was foreigners who showed greater interest in the upgrading and rescuing of local vernaculars' (1996: 52). Furthermore he draws attention to the influence of the Dutch theologian Kuyper's 'anti-liberal, neo-Calvinist Christian National Movement' on the President of the Genootskap, S.J. du Toit. For Pannevis' career in South Africa and his contribution to Afrikaans language and literature, see Geldenhuys 1967, Nienaber 1967, and Nienaber 1968, who shows that Pannevis taught S.J. du Toit privately, and not at the Gymnasium where Pannevis spent less than two (miserable) years (1968: 6-7).

30. Because of different political, economic and social issues in the Boer Republics (the Transvaal and the Orange Free State), the growth of Afrikaner identity and nationalism there assumed different features from that of the Cape, although there were obviously a number of important issues in common: language, religion, Roman-Dutch law and the same imperial power. The Transvaal's successful resistance of British annexation in 1880-1881, the discovery of gold in 1886 and the shift of the economic hub of southern Africa from the Cape to the Transvaal, the clash between President Paul Kruger's 'traditionalists' and the 'progressives', who were more tolerant of *uitlanders* (foreigners), the Jameson Raid, and the brutalizing effects of the South African War contributed to the formation of Afrikaner identities in the Republics (Giliomee 1987: 30-69). In this chapter I have focused exclusively on the Cape's classical tradition: there was (and still is) a classical tradition in the former Boer Republics, inextricably linked to the fight for the recognition and use of Afrikaans in cultural and academic circles.

31. Other Articles approved at the second meeting of the Association, included the rule that all members had to be Christians (Article VII) – the

minutes record that every meeting opened and closed with a prayer. If members resigned, they had to take the secrets of the Association to the grave with them (Article X) (Nienaber 1974: 53-4). Women were not permitted to be 'friends' of the Association (although this was disputed at one meeting); nor were they allowed to write articles for *Die Afrikaanse Patriot* (ibid.: *inleiding* (introduction)). Of the foundation members, three were teachers and three farmers: two were clergymen (Geldenhuys 1967: 34-5).

32. 'Class cleavages' and alliances were apparent in these organizations as well. The Afrikaner Bond was 'predominantly a populist movement which attracted the middling and small farmers', whilst Hofmeyr's ZABBV and the Afrikaner Bond drew on alliances formed between 'Afrikaner businessmen in the towns beyond Cape Town, the large landholders and commercial farmers' (Giliomee 1987: 39).

33. For the second Afrikaans language movement after the South African War, see Giliomee and Mbenga 2008: 228. By the outbreak of the First World War, Afrikaans-speaking nationalists were gaining control of the Dutch Reformed Church (Giliomee 1987: 67).

34. On his death, the Chairman of CASA sent a letter of condolence on behalf of the association to the Minister of Foreign Affairs who was also an Honorary Vice-President of the Classical Association (Henderson 2006: 136).

35. Gonin, Pistorius, Smuts (Stellenbosch); de Kock (Pretoria); Van Rooy (University of the Orange Free State).

36. Richards: *Gebed by Seneca, die Stoïsyn* (*AC* 8, 1965: 124); Smuts: *Die Etiek van Seneca* (*AC* 30, 1987: 1); de Kock *Die Kosmeet van Egipte* (*AClass* 39, 1996: 1); cf. Hugo *Calvyn en Seneca* (*AClass* 18, 1975: 2).

37. See the conference report in *AClass* 1, 1958: 164; for the official bilingualism, ibid:. 170, reaffirmed at the 1961 conference (Henderson 2005: 110).

38. Henderson 2004: 92; a concern of the 1959 conference too (ibid.: 100).

39. Henderson 2004: 94. For further contact between CASA and the Taalkommissie, see Henderson 2007: 112.

40. Interestingly, the Dutch scholars (Wagenvoort, Westendorp Boerma, and Enk) contributing to the journal chose to write in Latin, English and French.

41. Henderson 2004: 94-5; for fears (in 1963!) about the journal being 'too international', see Henderson 2005: 116; for the policy to review only works by local authors in the journal, see Henderson 2006: 139 (and the proposal, in 1968, 'to include a limited number of reviews of works by foreign classicists').

42. Hepple notes that, at the opening of Parliament in July 1958, only *'Die Stem'* ('The Voice'), the national anthem, was sung, without 'God Save the Queen' (1967: 129), even though South Africa was still a member of the Commonwealth.

43. For Haarhoff's intense friendship with Jackson Knight, the British Virgilian scholar, see Wiseman 1992: 178-206. Wiseman's compassionate account of Haarhoff's communications with Heraclitus, his belief that he was the reincarnation of Cornelius Gallus to Jackson Knight's Marcus Agrippa, his communications with Virgil via a medium (in German!) and then Virgil's dictations in Latin in response to queries about the interpretation and translation of the *Aeneid* make compelling reading.

44. Henderson 2004: 97; eventually (in 1969) the head of the obscure nymph Terina on a fifth-century stater was chosen as the association's emblem (Henderson 2006: 148). Why the head of a female figure from ancient Bruttium in southern Italy (Magna Graecia) should have been chosen is not clear, but it may have something to do with Haarhoffian notions of cultural fusion. He was still alive at the time.

45. van Groningen, visiting Dutch scholar from Leiden in 1963, gave his lectures at Stellenbosch in Afrikaans (Henderson 2005: 117).

46. Interestingly, CASA's records reflect the visits of British classicists invited by universities known for their opposition to the government's *apartheid* policies. e.g. the Students' Visiting Lecturers' Trust Fund and the Visiting Hofmeyr Fellow's fund at the University of the Witwatersrand (Henderson 2005: 112, 121; 2006: 148) and the Department of Drama at the University of Natal (Henderson 2006: 148).

47. CASA was finally admitted as a member of FIEC in 1961 (Henderson 2005: 111).

48. See n. 34 above. The list of Patrons and Honorary Vice-Presidents of CASA in 1961 is a lesson in political expediency and academic protectionism: the Chief Justice of South Africa, the High Commissioner for the Union of South Africa in the UK and the Ambassadors of Greece and Italy (Henderson 2005: 111). So too the list of those invited to one of CASA's conferences (Henderson 2006: 153).

49. Northern Regional Branch, later the Transvaal Regional Organization (Potchefstroom, 1956); Southern Regional Branch/South-Western Cape, later the Western Cape Regional Organization (Cape Town/Stellenbosch, formally established in 1963) (Henderson 2004: 91, 2005: 116, 118); Orange Free State (Bloemfontein, 1959); Eastern Cape Branch (Grahamstown, 1960), (Henderson 2004: 108); Natal Branch (Botha's Hill, 1967), Port Elizabeth Branch (1967) (Henderson 2006: 142). For lively branch activities, ranging from teachers' conferences to readings of Latin verse, attempting to stimulate interest in Latin in white schools, see Henderson 2004: 107-8; 2005: 121; 2006: 140-4; 2007: 104-5, 113.

50. For Viljoen's concerns, in 1958, about the introduction of an African language as a third language for matriculation, see Henderson 2004: 93. For proposals to abolish the Latin requirement for lawyers in 1957 and 1968, see Henderson 2005: 110; 2006: 138. For the strategic support of the Chief Justice in 1968, see Henderson 2006, 138, 146. For CASA's proposals (in 1973) to make representations to the Association of Law Societies in order to retain the Latin requirement, see Henderson 2007: 109. For meetings in the OFS (in 1973) between CASA and the local law society, Henderson 2007: 111.

51. Henderson 2004: 100. For similar publicity for Classics, see Henderson 2004: 99 (White's radio talks on classical subjects in 1957); Henderson 2004: 105 (the special edition of *Lantern* focusing on Greece and Rome), Henderson 2005: 140 (a well-attended Latin Reading Competition).

52. Henderson records that in 1957 the numbers of matriculants taking Latin in Transvaal schools alone had almost doubled and the number of schools offering the subject in that province had risen from 45 to 77 (2004: 98). These

statistics are re-interpreted in 1959 when a school inspector notes that the percentage of Latin candidates during the previous decade dropped from 20.6% to 15.9% of the total number of candidates (ibid.: 107 n. 89). Cf. Behr and Macmillan 1966: 172 for the decline in percentages of Latin candidates during the period 1957-1963.

53. For the gradual decline in Latin as a school subject, see Henderson 2005: 109; 2006: 137; 142-3; 2007: 106, 108. Smuts, writing in 1976, lamented the disappearance of Greek from high schools and the 'drastic' decline in the number of schools offering Latin (1976: 19). CASA in fact commissioned the Human Sciences Research Council to investigate the position of Latin in secondary schools, a report which was finally published, only in Afrikaans, in 1984. The report, which includes comparisons with the status of Latin in high schools in England, France, West Germany, Canada and the USA (as if these are the countries with which South Africa should compare itself) makes chilling reading: the numbers of matriculants in Latin decline from 2, 246 in 1974 to 772 in 1980, spread over 153 schools of all races (state and private), suggesting Latin matriculation classes of about five students per school (Weideman 1984: 141-2). Interestingly, Weideman reports that 75.8% of these students are at English-speaking schools (ibid.: 140).

54. Behr and Macmillan 1966: 216. The University of Transkei was estab-lished in 1976 at the request of the apartheid-constituted 'homeland' government of the Transkei.

55. With the singular exception of Henderson's *obiter dictum* on the state of emergency in Rhodesia (1959), when discussing proposals for a combined conference with the Central African Classical Association in Salisbury (now Harare, Zimbabwe) (2004: 105). 1959 in South Africa was hardly uneventful.

56. With the notable exception of Dr Banda's Malawi (courted by the *apart-heid* regime) which boasted the extraordinary Kamuzu Academy (opened in 1981) in which Latin, Greek and Ancient History were taught by British ex-patriates to the brightest pupils in the country (*Akroterion* 26 (4) 1981: 45; 33 (4)1988: 142-3). The author recalls Dr Banda informing a cheering crowd in Blantyre that no-one was educated without a study of the Classics. CASA seemed to need this kind of ammunition in the 1980s.

57. The first so to do. She was Lydia Baumbach, then a lecturer at Rhodes University in Grahamstown, later Professor and Head of Classics at the Uni-versity of Cape Town (1982-1987) and the first woman to chair CASA (1983-1984). Two other women have chaired the association: Louise Cilliers (1991-1994) and Ann Mackay (1998-2000). Atkinson notes that, when Baum-bach joined the Department of Greek at the University of Pretoria, she 'shocked the more conservative fathers of the Classical Association by giving a public lecture on the U.P. campus in English' (in 1964!) (1991: 2). CASA's gender politics have been shaped (predictably) by the intersecting discourses of Afri-kaner and English colonial patriarchies.

58. 13% of total number of articles published – authors include Smuts, van Rooy, Haarhoff, Naudé, de Kock, Conradie, Erasmus, Holm, Linde and Louw. The decline thereafter is significant. 1968-1977: 9%; 1978-1987: 9%; 1988-1997: 3%; 1998-2007: 2.2%. The decline reflects the waning of Afrikaner nationalist

ardour and the decline in the numbers of Afrikaans-speaking classicists prepared to publish in Afrikaans to the possible detriment of their careers.

59. 1958-1967: 46%; 1968-1977: 100%; 1978-1987: 50%; 1988-1997: 50%;
1998-2007: 33.3%.

60. Appreciations: Haarhoff (Petrie 1958: 9-13), Petrie (Steven 1959: 7-10),
Naudé (Gonin 1977: vii; colleagues and friends 1977: viii-xi; Rosen 1977: xii-xv),
Gonin (Smuts 1981: x-xiii; van Warmelo 1981: xiv), Atkinson (Wardle 2005:
vii-xi), Conradie (Claassen 2008: ix-xii). The appreciation for Naudé, written in
Latin by Gonin, was published when Gonin was managing editor of *Acta
Classica* and Naudé on the editorial committee; the appreciation for Gonin,
written in Afrikaans by Smuts, was published when Gonin was still managing
editor of the journal, as he was for eighteen years (1967-1984). Obituaries:
Steven (van Rooij 1962: 1-2), Bruwer (Smuts 1985: 1-4), Whiteley (Matier 1986:
1-2), Smuts (Conradie 1987: 1-3), Benadé (Richards 1988: 1-3), Goodyear (Hall
1988: 5-11), van der Walt (Swanepoel 1989: 1-2), Baumbach (Paap 1991: 1-3:
Chadwick 1991: 3-5), de Kock (Henderson 1996: 1-3), Gonin (Kriel 1997: 1-3),
van Rooy (Lombard 1998: 1-3), Vogel-Weidemann (1999), Mezzabotta (Whitaker 2000: 1-3), Naudé (Saddington 2001: 1-3), van Stekelenburg (Claassen
2003: 1-4).

61. Smuts (Conradie 1987), de Kock (Henderson 1996), Gonin (Kriel 1997),
van Rooy (Lombard 1998), Naudé (Saddington 2001).

62. Formerly the Classical Newsletter, the creation of the indefatigable
Francois Smuts of the Latin Department at the University of Stellenbosch,
Akroterion developed into a quarterly in 1970, edited by a committee headed by
Smuts. The journal was designed to publish articles of general interest in the
Classics, especially helpful to Latin teachers, *varia didactica*, reports of CASA's
branches and at least one article of scholarly merit in each issue. When the
journal became accepted for subsidy purposes by the Department of National
Education in 1987, the journal gradually lost its chatty, informative tone and
became a sober younger sister of *Acta Classica*. With the virtual disappearance
of Latin in the schools, the articles acquired more *gravitas* and the four annual
issues were reduced to one in 1998. As the journal is published by a predominantly Afrikaans-speaking university, it is unsurprising that, in the period
1970-2007, 35% of the articles published are in Afrikaans. Interestingly, before
1987, 42% of all articles published were in Afrikaans; after 1987 and the
acceptance of the journal for subsidy purposes, the percentage of articles
written in Afrikaans declines to 27%.

63. 55% of the total. Milne, Rhodes University (Baumbach 1972: 35),
Petrie, University of Natal (Smuts, Clarence 1980: 1-6), Shillington, Univer-
sity of the Witwatersrand (Shillington 1980: 30-1), Henderson, University of
Natal (Murgatroyd 1981: 1-3), Farrer, University of Natal (Bredenkamp
1982: 160), Whiteley, University of Natal (Matier 1986: 35-6), Whiteford,
University of Cape Town (Baumbach 1987: 48), Goodyear, University of the
Witwatersrand (Saddington 1987: 74), Hewitt, Rhodes University (Jackson
1989: 160-1), Bristowe, University of Natal (Gosling 1989: 208), Cartwright,
Rustenburg Girls' High School (O'Dowd 1993: 96), Jorge, University of the
Western Cape (Atkinson 1995: 92), Gosling, University of KwaZulu-Natal

(Hilton 2008: 3-6). Whiteley and Goodyear also appear in *Acta Classica* (see n. 60).

64. Only one English-speaking classicist receives an appreciation in *Akroterion* – Mezzabotta (Whitaker 2000: 1) – which can at times be astonishingly parochial. See the obituary for de Villiers (Smuts 1976: 40-1) and the series of fraternal *laudationes* exchanged between Smuts (Professor of Latin at the University of Stellenbosch) and van Rensburg (Professor of Greek at the same university) below. Appreciations/tributes: van Rensburg (Smuts 1971: 1-6), Smuts (van Rensburg 1976: 1-2), van Rensburg (Smuts 1976: 1-2), Gonin (Meiring 1977: 30-1), Smuts (Baumbach 1981: 43), Smuts (Baumbach 1983: 61-2), Kriel (Mans 1984: 32), Postma (Postma 1989: 251-3), Conradie (Thom 1996: 2-4).

65. 'Recent judgments' refer to decisions by the Natal and Transvaal Supreme Courts in 1981 and 1982 to grant admission to the Bar two applicants who had completed a preliminary or introductory Latin course at university, rather than Latin 1, previously interpreted as one year of post-matriculation Latin at tertiary level. See van Stekelenburg 1982: 89.

66. See Mackay (1999: 79-90) for the gloomy overall picture in Classics departments at South African universities. A decade later, nothing has come of the imaginative 'way forward' proposed by Mackay. Cf. Henderson's earlier compilation of statistics (1986: 2-12) in order to appreciate the extent of the decline. Scourfield's analysis of the future of the Classics in post-*apartheid* South Africa has proved prophetic (1993: 43-54).

67. Perhaps one of the symptoms of this is the sudden rise in the number of English-speaking CASA chairs in the period 1995-2007: Whitaker (1995-1996), Scourfield (1997), Mackay (1998-2000), Atkinson (2001-2002), Hilton (2005-2007). Furthermore, two of these (Scourfield, Mackay) were foreign nationals. In the formative years of the Association (1956-1976), Farrer was the sole English-speaking classicist to be elected CASA chair (1965-1968).

68. For a biography of Viljoen, see Gastrow 1992: 317-19. See too Martin's obituary in *The Times* published on 5 April, 2009 and accessed at http://www.thetimes.co.za/PrintEdition/Insight?Article.aspx?id=974188 on 8 May 2009.

2. The Classics and English-speaking
South African Identities

1. *Carm.* 3.30 ('*Exegi monumentum* ...'). Rhodes, keenly conscious of his legacy, quoted the words *non omnis moriar* ('I shall not altogether perish') in a postscript to his 1893 will (Rotberg 1988: 665-6).

2. Wardle 1993: 86. The *Meditations* were under Rhodes's pillow when he died (Hilton and Gosling 2007: 21). Rotberg also includes Seneca, Epictetus and Plutarch among the classical texts which had interested Rhodes since his youth (1988: 384). At Oxford, he was remembered as being interested in Plato, Aristotle and Thucydides (ibid.: 91, 95).

3. On a visit to England in 1888 to negotiate a Royal Charter for the British South Africa Company, which he obtained in 1889, Rhodes conceived of the

translation project (Wardle 1993: 86). The actual conception of the translation project is thus closely linked to the implementation of Rhodes's imperialist designs (i.e. the formation of the company).

4. Tamarkin (1996) is especially good on Rhodes's premiership and his courting of the Afrikaner Bond. In fact, Tamarkin uses the imagery of courtship, marriage and divorce in order to characterise this tragic relationship. For Rhodes's support of Hofmeyr's bill (1882) permitting the use of Dutch in the Cape parliament, see Tamarkin 1996: 88; for Rhodes's *volte face* (1886) on the excise duty on Cape spirits, ibid.: 88, 96; for his attack on the non-racial franchise (1887), ibid.: 97.

5. During his premiership, Rhodes voted for the Strop Bill, which permitted black servants to be flogged (Tamarkin 1996: 140), again for the Masters and Servants Bill (ibid.: 156), supported the Bond's view on the 'native policy' (ibid.: 175), pushed through parliament the notorious Glen Grey Act of 1894, which disenfranchised many Black voters and created a labour 'reserve' (ibid.: 197-8), and accepted amendments to his own Scab Act which had aroused the ire of Afrikaner sheep farmers, who resented the interference of the modernist state in their traditional farming techniques (ibid.: 209). On the Glen Grey 'Experiment', see Giliomee and Mbenga 2008: 187.

6. See Tamarkin 1996: 215: 'Coming to his home, where he used to entertain many of them, Cape Afrikaners were impressed and captivated not only by the Englishman who manifested love for their artistic heritage, but also by his openness, warmth and hospitality'. For Rhodes's interest in Cape Dutch furniture, see Williams 1938: 221-2.

7. For the Jameson Raid and its effect on his relationship with Hofmeyr and the Bond, see Tamarkin 1996: 238-304. For Rhodes's interest in the Classics at school, see Rotberg 1988: 31-2; for his intermittent career at Oxford, firstly at University College, which rejected him, and then Oriel (1873-1881), ibid.: 84-107.

8. A year after Rhodes' first term at Oxford, a Tory government led by Disraeli replaced that of Gladstone's Liberals (1874). Disraeli's imperialist ideals, and those of Ruskin at Oxford, clearly influenced the intellectual atmosphere at the university and in its many clubs, which fostered the notion of the superiority of the Anglo-Saxon race, and the innate rectitude of the British Empire, certainly the salvation of Africa from its savagery (see Rotberg 1988: 90-107). It was Disraeli who authorized the annexation of the Transvaal in 1877. See Hingley 2007: 137 for Oxford University as the 'key centre for the education of administrators for the Indian Civil Service during the late nineteenth and early twentieth centuries, where classics featured prominently in the entry examination'. See too Vasunia 2005: 49: 'In the years from 1888-1905, for instance, three successive viceroys of India came from Balliol College alone ...'. For classics at Oxford in the nineteenth century, see Stray 2007: 13.

9. See Vasunia 2005: 38-64; Hingley 2007: 137. Vasunia skilfully demonstrates how British authors of the Victorian and Edwardian eras 'legitimised their own empire through the turn to ancient Rome' (ibid.: 39).

10. Rhodes belonged to the same club (the very chic Bullingdon Polo Club) as Oscar Wilde, but there is no evidence that the two actually met (Rotberg 1988:

85, 90; Maylam 2005: 98). It was in clubs such as these that Rhodes made important social and political connections – clearly the function of club membership for him.

11. Paton's biography of Hofmeyr (1964) is, in my opinion, unsurpassed, and contains some very perceptive analyses of Hofmeyr's problematic relationship with his mother and its effect on his sexuality and his career.

12. Hofmeyr's interference (and that of his moralistic mother) in the private life of the Dean of the Faculty of Medicine, who was suspected of conducting an extra-marital affair, for which he was wrongfully dismissed from the academic staff, resulted in a prolonged stand-off between the University Senate, the Council and the young Principal (Paton 1964: 96-106). Even his boyhood friend, Haarhoff, opposed him (ibid.: 103, 108).

13. For Hofmeyr's friendship with Haarhoff which began in their schooldays, see Paton 1964: 10, 14-15, 30, 43, 55-6. Hofmeyr was particularly interested in Augustus and his attempts to reconcile *imperium* and *libertas* – an interesting foreshadowing of his later political beliefs; in 1929, before his conversion from white racist thinking, Hofmeyr favourably compared Augustus with Mussolini (ibid.: 92-3, 156).

14. For Hertzog's political strategy – to use the coalition to facilitate obtaining two-thirds of the votes of a joint sitting of the House of Assembly and the Senate in order to abolish the Cape black African franchise and so pave the way for the infamous Hertzog Bills of 1935, see Higgs 1997: 115-16, 121.

15. The United Party coalition split in 1939 over the question of South African participation in the Second World War (on Britain's side). Hertzog, the Prime Minister, opted for neutrality, but in the House of Assembly, persuaded by Smuts, a majority of thirteen votes, in favour of participation in the war, won. Smuts then served his second term as Prime Minister (1939-1948) (see Higgs 1997: 130). Many Nationalist Afrikaners, most of whom were pro-Nazi and anti-Semitic, bitterly opposed South Africa's participation in the war on the British side.

16. Hofmeyr had been one of eleven MPs opposed to Hertzog's Representation of Natives in Parliament Bill (Higgs 1997: 147). Professor Jabavu (see Chapter 3) wrote to thank Hofmeyr for his opposition to the Bill (ibid.: 124). See too Paton 1964: 232.

17. Haarhoff was offered the Rectorship of the University College of the Orange Free State in 1944, 'but was forced to refuse, due to political opposition from the Nationalists and the Broederbond' (Whitaker 1997: 7).

18. This perception was based on the premise that most Afrikaans-speaking classicists had specialized in one language (Greek or Latin) to the detriment of the other, in contrast to the Oxonian tradition which stressed competence of a high level in both. The 'tribal colleges', now considered a derogatory term by the ruling élite, some of whom were educated at them, focussed primarily on introductory courses in Hellenistic Greek and legal Latin, largely in order to satisfy professional requirements.

19. Similarly, Chapman's allusions, in the same year as Raven's inaugural, to parallels between ancient Sparta and *apartheid* South Africa in an article published in *Concept*, the magazine of the Convocation of the University of

Natal (1973: 28-32). The use of Sparta by South African classicists, both liberal and conservative, would in itself make a fascinating study.

20. See *NUX* 7, 22 June 1972: 1 (*NUX* was the students' newspaper of the then University of Natal, Pietermaritzburg, now the University of KwaZulu-Natal, where it is still published).

21. See *NUX* 6, 8 June 1972: 2, 7-8; *NUX* 7, 22 June 1972: 1, 6; *NUX* 8, 10 August 1972: 3; cf. the article 'Black campuses in turmoil', *NUX* 4, 12 May 1972: 1. For the fate of the 318 students from UCT, who were arrested, see *NUX* 2, 8 March 1973: 7 – one was found guilty of contravening a municipal by-law and fined; in Pietermaritzburg, nineteen students were arrested, of whom three were brought to court and found not guilty. The Minister of Police was required to pay damages to eleven UCT students and a janitor who were 'allegedly' assaulted (*NUX* 2, 14 March 1974: 1).

22. For the use of 'detribalization' (supported by the missionaries) and 'retribalization' (favoured by Hertzog's regime) in South African political discourse, see Higgs 1997: 54, 60. Cf. Chipkin 2007: 28-9.

23. See Lambert 1989: 19-23. The title of the article 'The Classics: A Bridge between the Worlds' refers to the potential of the study of the Classics to bridge the first and third world divides and clearly reflects the *zeitgeist* of the period.

24. In this account I have avoided the complicated internal politics of the monastery during its early history. For the controversies surrounding Trappist Rule (especially the vow of silence) and evangelization, for the role of the Missionary Sisters of the Precious Blood, and for the formation of the Religious Missionaries of Mariannhill, see Brain 2002: 82-7. Green's historical novel, *For the Sake of Silence* (2008), based on many years of painstaking research, is especially interesting.

25. Rhodes too spent his first years in South Africa in Natal – working, with his brother, on a cotton plantation in the Umkomaas Valley (Rotberg 1988: 44-54), before he was seduced by the prospect of digging for diamonds.

26. For the revival of the Nomkhubulwane rituals, see Lambert 2008: 545-53.

27. See Caroline Alexander's interesting article on teaching Homer's *Odyssey* in Malawi during the years 1982-1985, and the subsequent appropriation of elements in the *Odyssey* by the Malawian oral tradition (1991: 53).

3. The Classics and Black South African Identities

1. Colleagues at the University of Cape Town and the University of Stellenbosch, who have been members of the Western Cape branch of the Classical Association of South Africa for many years, have confirmed how this branch succeeded (especially in the 1980s) in enabling 'non-white' (i.e. 'Coloured' and Chinese) Latin teachers to become members of the Association or attend meetings, without the knowledge of the central committee of CASA, which adhered to the government's whites-only policies (personal communication).

2. For his opinion of Jabavu, see Mandela 1994: 42; for Mandela's career at Fort Hare and his subsequent studies at Unisa and the University of the

Witwatersrand, where he was the only black student in the law faculty, see 1994: 48-50, 64, 82-3, 137-8.

3. Although D.D.T. Jabavu's degree was in English, he studied Latin in London and taught it at a British primary school (Queen Mary's Grammar School), while studying for his teaching diploma in Birmingham (Higgs 1997: 20, 29).

4. In 1883, the year before the first edition of the newspaper appeared, John Tengo Jabavu passed the matriculation examination for which Latin was a requirement – the second black African in the Cape Colony to achieve this (Higgs 1997: 174 n.67; de Kock 1996: 116).

5. Before the establishment of the University of Fort Hare, a number of black South Africans were sent to black colleges in the USA, such as Lincoln, Howard, Wilberforce and Tuskegee (Burchell 1976: 66-7) (cf. the migration of the sons of Dutch colonists in the Cape to universities in the Netherlands). In fact, this migration, which often resulted in the development of the kind of political awareness perceived as threatening to conservative white South Africans, resulted in government support for the establishment of the South African Native College (later Fort Hare), the opening of which was attended by the Prime Minister of the Union, General Louis Botha (Higgs 1997: 34). For D.D.T. Jabavu's visit to Tuskegee in 1913 and the effect of Booker T. Washington's project, especially the Agriculture Department, on his educational ideas, see Higgs 1997: 23-8. At Fort Hare, Jabavu's teaching of Latin (and Bantu Studies, Anthropology, History, Bantu Languages and Law) was always combined with practical, vocational training: for his contribution to the Native Farmers' Association, see Higgs 1997: 37-42. cf. Giliomee and Mbenga 2008: 287.

6. Approximately a quarter of Cape Town's population of 45,000 (by the mid-1870s) has been estimated to have been racially mixed 'and other' (Christison 2007: 202). Why Robert Grendon and his brother, William, were boarders at Zonnebloem, when his father and [white] step-mother lived nearby, obviously reflected the racist *mores* of bourgeois Cape Town society and tensions within the family itself. Robert, William and their elder sister, Mary Ann, were the 'coloured' offspring of their father's first marriage (ibid.: 202-3). Canon Peters was proud of the non-racial character of Zonnebloem, which enrolled white, black and 'coloured students' (ibid.: 213).

7. John Langalibalele Dube (1871-1946) founded the Zulu Christian Industrial School at Ohlange (near Durban), where the newspaper *Ilanga lase Natal* was published and where Robert Grendon was headteacher from 1903-1905, during Dube's absence abroad. Dube too had visited (and been impressed and inspired by) Booker T. Washington's Tuskegee Institute (see n. 5 above). In 1912, Dube became the first President of the South African Native National Congress, later the African National Congress (Christison 2007: 521-2). Grendon had been the impressive headmaster of the Native Training Institute at Edendale, near Pietermaritzburg (1900-1903), before his career at Ohlange (ibid.: 485-7).

8. *Paul Kruger's Dream* is not the only poem by Grendon to be profoundly influenced by his classical education. His incomplete *Pro Aliis Damnati* (2,742 lines) (1904-1905) is replete with references to ancient Greek literature (drama,

the novel, pastoral poetry) as well as Renaissance literature. The names of some of the characters in this love epic are carefully chosen: Helen, Memnon, Damon, Cleon, Dikidion. The name of Helen's husband, Zenzema, and the geographical setting, root the poem in a South African context (Christison 2007: 649-706).

9. Higgs notes that when white members of the South African Communist Party attempted to speak at Fort Hare in 1933, 'they were barred from the campus and students were forbidden to attend CPSA meetings held in nearby villages' (1997: 47). Apparently, the communists pitched a tent on a nearby hill and some students sneaked out to meet them. By the time Hani was at Fort Hare, the Suppression of Communism Act had been used extensively to silence opposition to the *apartheid* regime (especially during the infamous Treason Trials of 1956-1961, which form some of the background to Hani's career at Fort Hare).

10. http://www.anc.org.za/people/hani c.html, accessed 19 June 2009. Claassen (1993), in attempting to rebut the argument that the study of Latin is an elitist pursuit, speculates about what Hani would have gained from his Latin studies, which would have contributed to his fight for freedom and justice in South Africa, and makes some interesting analogies between Roman and South African socio-political history. See Klaaste 1995: 16 for Claassen's letter to the press reclaiming Jugurtha, Hannibal, Augustine, Jerome and Lactantius for our shared African heritage. Klaaste's comments are worth noting: 'I am now being supported by Afrikaner academics in, among other things, rewriting African history so as to supplant the slave mentality with nobility.'

11. Higgs 1997: 91-3; in this respect, note Jabavu's friendship with Sauer, a 'liberal' Cape Afrikaner, who eventually became Minister of Native Affairs and supported the Cape's non-racial franchise. Jabavu's son wrote a letter of congratulations to Hofmeyr on his stand against the Hertzog Bills (see Chapter 2; Paton 1964: 232).

12. See the attitude of a visiting Oxford don, Margery Perham, to Jabavu's liberalism in 1929, which she found positively 'dangerous' (Higgs 1997: 110-11).

13. Conversely, de Kock notes in the narratives of the well-known white missionary couple, Robert and Mary Moffat, their reluctance to admit to the inevitable Africanization of their European identities in South Africa: '... just as African missionary subjects at Lovedale existed in an agonistic relation to the identities prescribed for them by the metanarrative of civilization, so one detects in the narratives of the Moffats some revealing indications of what they most sought to silence and deny: their own Africanization' (1996: 155).

14. Cf. Dhlomo's comments on ancient Greek drama and the relationship of its genesis to that of contemporary African drama (1939). Attwell characterises his movement between affirmation of the 'underlying unity of African and European forms' and the 'unity of distinctively African traditions' as a reflection of the 'Janus-faced orientation of all cultural nationalism' (2005: 94).

15. As far as I am aware, the extent of the influence of Vergil's *Eclogues* and *Georgics* on the romantic and pastoral poetry of Vilakazi has never been fully assessed.

Conclusion

1. For Coetzee's spelling of Mariannhill with one 'n' as a deliberate fictional strategy, rather than a simple spelling mistake, see Green 2005: 2-3.

2. The published version of the lesson I used was the Secker and Warburg 2003 version with the 'Australian ending'. For the various earlier published versions and the effect of the 'Australian ending', see Green 2005: 9-10.

Bibliography

Alexander, C., 'An Ideal State', *New Yorker* (16 December 1991), 53.

Althusser, L., *Essays on Ideology* (Verso, 1984).

Ashcroft, B., Griffiths, G. & Tiffin, H. *The Post-Colonial Studies Reader* (Routledge, 1995).

Atkinson, J., '*In Memoriam*: Professor Lydia Baumbach', *Akroterion* 36 (1/2, 1991), 2-4.

Atkinson, J.E., '*In Memoriam* Diane Jorge', *Akroterion* 40 (2, 1995), 61-3.

Attwell, D., *Rewriting Modernity* (University of KwaZulu-Natal Press, 2005).

Bartky, S.L., 'Foucault, Femininity, and the Modernization of Patriarchal Power', in I. Diamond & L. Quinby (eds), *Feminism and Foucault* (Northeastern University Press, 1988), 61-86.

Baumbach, L., '*In Memoriam*: Andrew Milne. 1.12.1890-11.7.1972', *Akroterion* 17 (2/3, 1972), 35.

Baumbach, L., '*In Memoriam* André Malan Hugo', *Acta Classica* (1975), 1-4.

Baumbach, L., '*Laudatio*', *Akroterion* 26 (4, 1981), 43.

Baumbach, L., 'Prof. Frans Smuts: 'N Huldeblyk', *Akroterion* 28 (3/4, 1983), 61-2.

Baumbach, L., '*In Memoriam* Professor Frans Smuts: 1 April 1916-27 Maart 1987', *Akroterion* 32 (2, 1987), 46-7.

Baumbach, L., *In Memoriam*: Robin Whiteford', *Akroterion* 32 (2, 1987), 48.

Behr, A.L., *Three Centuries of Coloured Education* (unpublished D.Ed. thesis, Potchefstroom University for C.H.E., 1952).

Behr, A.L., *New Perspectives in South African Education* (Butterworths, 1984).

Behr, A.L. & Macmillan, R.G., *Education in South Africa* (van Schaik, 1966).

Bloomberg, C., *Christian Nationalism and the Rise of the Afrikaner Broederbond in South Africa, 1914-1948* (Macmillan, 1990).

Bouillon, A. (ed.), *Immigration africaine en Afrique du Sud* (Karthala, 1999).

Brain, J. *The Catholic Church in Natal over 150 years* (Missionary Oblates of Mary Immaculate, 2002).

Bredenkamp, V., 'Bernard Farrer – a Tribute', *Akroterion* 72 (3/4, 1982), 160 [copied from the *Natal Witness*, 26 August 1982].

Bryant, A.T., *The Zulu People As They Were Before The White Man Came* (Shuter and Shooter, 1949).

Burchell, D.E., 'African Higher Education and the Establishment of the South African Native College, Fort Hare', *South African Historical Journal* 8 (1976), 60-83.

Cairns, D. & Liapis, V. (eds), *Dionysalexandros: Essays on Aeschylus and his Fellow Tragedians in Honour of Alexander F. Garvie* (Classical Press of Wales, 2006).

Chadwick, J., 'Lydia Baumbach's Contribution to Mycenaean Studies', *Acta Classica* 34 (1991), 3-5.

Chapman, G.A., 'A Traditional Way of Life (Sparta – The Military Machine)', *Concept* 4 (1973), 28-32.

Chapman, G.A., *Women in Early Greek Comedy: Fact, Fantasy and Feminism* (University of Natal Press, 1985).

Chipkin, I., *Do South Africans Exist? Nationalism, Democracy and the Identity of 'The People'* (Wits University Press, 2007).

151

Bibliography

Christison, G., *African Jerusalem: The Vision of Robert Grendon* (unpublished Ph.D. thesis, University of KwaZulu-Natal, Pietermaritzburg, 2007).

Cilliers, L., '*In Memoriam* Elbert Lucas (Tot) de Kock 1924-1996', *Akroterion* 42 (1, 1997), 2-3.

Claassen, J-M., 'Chris Hani and the Classics', *Sunday Nation*, August 22 (1993).

Claassen, J-M., 'Editorial', *Akroterion* 40 (2, 1995), 61-3.

Claassen, J-M., '*In Memoriam* Albert Victor (Bert) Van Stekelenburg 31.03.1940-11.03.2003', *Acta Classica* 46 (2003), 1-4.

Claassen, J-M., 'Pieter Jacobus Conradie: An Appreciation', *Acta Classica* 51 (2008), ix-xii.

Clarence, D., 'Tribute to Alexander Petrie at the memorial service held in Pietermaritzburg on Tuesday, 11 December 1979', *Akroterion* 25 (1, 1980), 4-6 [preceded by an introduction by Smuts and a copy of Petrie's reflections on old age].

Coetzee, J.M., *Elizabeth Costello* (Secker & Warburg, 2003).

Conacher, D.J., *Aeschylus The Earlier Plays and Related Studies* (University of Toronto Press, 1996).

Conradie, P., '*In Memoriam* Francois Smuts', *Acta Classica* (1987), 1-3.

Davenport, T.R.H., *South Africa: A Modern History* (Macmillan, 1991, 4th edn).

De Kock, L., 'Reading History as Cultural Text', *Alternation* 2 (1, 1995), 65-78.

De Kock, L., *Civilising Barbarians: Missionary Narrative and African Textual Response in Nineteenth-Century South Africa* (Witwatersrand University Press/Lovedale Press, 1996).

Delanty, G., *Challenging Knowledge: the University in the knowledge society* (Open University Press, 2001).

[Editors], 'A Report on the Classical Association of South Africa, 1956-1957', *Acta Classica* 1 (1958), 164-9.

[Editors], 'A Report on the Classical Association of South Africa, February 1959-February 1961', *Acta Classica* 4 (1961), 117-23.

Els, J.M., 'The Course in Classical Culture at Fort Hare', *Akroterion* 39 (3/4, 1994), 164-8.

Evans, R., 'Perspectives on Post-Colonialism in South Africa: The Voortrekker Monument's Classical Heritage', in L. Hardwick & C. Gillespie (eds), *Classics in Post-Colonial Worlds* (Oxford, 2007), 141-56.

Fanon, F., *Black Skin, White Masks* (Pluto, 1986).

Forrest, W.G., 'Themistokles and Argos', *Classical Quarterly* 10 (1960), 221-41.

Foucault, M., *La volonté de savoir* (Gallimard, 1976).

Foxhall, L., 'Pandora Unbound: A Feminist Critique of Foucault's *History of Sexuality*', in D.H.J. Larmour, T.A. Miller & C. Platter (eds), *Rethinking Sexuality: Foucault and Classical Antiquity* (Princeton University Press, 1998), 122-37.

Gantz, T., 'Love and Death in the *Suppliants* of Aischylos', *Phoenix* 32 (4, 1978), 279-87.

Gastrow, S., *Who's Who in South African Politics Number 4* (Ravan Press, 1992).

Geldenhuys, D.J.C., *Pannevis en Preller met hul pleidooie* (Voortrekker Press, 1967).

Gevisser, M., *The Dream Deferred: Thabo Mbeki* (Jonathan Ball, 2007).

Giliomee, H., 'The Beginnings of Afrikaner Nationalism 1870-1915', in *South Africa in the Nineteenth Century* (University of South Africa Reader, 1987), 27-80.

Giliomee, H. & Mbenga, B., *New History of South Africa* (Tafelberg, 2008).

Goff, B. (ed.), *Classics and Colonialism* (Duckworth, 2005).

Gonin, H., 'Caroli P.T. Naudé In Honorem', *Acta Classica* 20 (1977), vii.

Gosling, A., '*In Memoriam*: Barbara Bristowe', *Akroterion* 34 (3/4, 1989), 208.

Green, M., 'Deplorations' [on J.M. Coetzee's 'The Humanities in Africa'], *English Studies Research Seminar* 14 April (2005), 1-24 (unpublished).

Green, M. Cawood, *For the Sake of Silence* (Umuzi, 2008).

Grové, J., 'J.P.J. van Rensburg – soos 'n oud-student hom sien', *Akroterion* 21 (4, 1976), 40-2.

Gultong, G. (ed.), *The Cambridge Companion to Foucault* (Cambridge University Press, 1994).

Haarhoff, T.J., *The Stranger at the Gate* (Longmans, 1938).

Haarhoff, T.J. & van den Heever, C.M., *The Achievement of Afrikaans* (CNA, 1934).

Hall, E., *Inventing the Barbarian: Greek Self-Definition through Tragedy* (Clarendon Press, 1989).

Hall, E., Macintosh F. & Wrigley, A. (eds), *Dionysus Since 69* (Oxford University Press, 2004).

Hall, J.M., *Ethnic Identity in Greek Antiquity* (Cambridge University Press, 1997).

Hammerschlag, T., *Aeschylus' The Suppliants* (Judy Daish (agent), 1999).

Hardwick, L., 'Contests and Continuities in Classical Traditions: African Migrations', in J. Hilton & A. Gosling (eds), *Alma Parens Originalis? The Receptions of Classical Literature and Thought in Africa, Europe, the United States, and Cuba* (Peter Lang, 2007), 43-71.

Hardwick. L. & Gillespie, C. (eds), *Classics in Post-Colonial Worlds* (Oxford, 2007).

Hardwick, L. & Stray, C. (eds), *A Companion to Classical Receptions* (Blackwell Publishing, 2008).

Heath, M., 'The "Social Function" of Tragedy: Clarifications and Questions', in D. Cairns & V. Liapis (eds), *Dionysalexandros: Essays on Aeschylus and his Fellow Tragedians in Honour of Alexander F. Garvie* (Classical Press of Wales, 2006), 253-81.

Hemmy, G., *De Promontorio Bonae Spei* (tr. & ed. K.D. White, South African Public Library, 1959).

Hemmy, G., *De Testimoniis* (tr. & ed. M.L. Hewett, Rustica Press, 1998).

Henderson, M.M., *Alcibiades and the Ancient Historian* (University of Natal Press, 1979).

Henderson, W.J., 'Classical Statistics', *Akroterion* 31 (1, 1986), 2-12.

Henderson, W.J., 'South Africa. Greek and Latin Philology', in G. Arrighetti *et al.* (eds), *La filologia greca e Latina nel secolo XX* (Pisa, 1989).

Henderson, W.J., '*In Memoriam* Elbert Lucas (Tot) de Kock 19.10.1924-30.01.1996', *Acta Classica* 39 (1996) 1-3.

Henderson, W.J., 'The Classical Association of South Africa: April 1956-January 1961', *Akroterion* 49 (2004), 89-109.

Henderson, W.J., 'The Classical Association of South Africa: February 1961-July 1966', *Akroterion* 50 (2005), 109-23.

Henderson, W.J., 'The Classical Association of South Africa: July 1966-January 1971', *Akroterion* 51 (2006), 135-56.

Henderson, W.J., 'The Classical Association of South Africa: January 1971-January 1975', *Akroterion* 52 (2007), 99-114.

Henderson, W.J., 'The Classical Association of South Africa: January 1975-January 1979', *Akroterion* 53 (2008), 81-97.

Hepple, A., *Verwoerd* (Penguin, 1967).

Hewett, M.L. (tr. & ed.), Hemmy, *De Testimoniis* (Rustica Press, 1998).

Higgs, C., *The Ghost of Equality: The Public Lives of D.D.T. Jabavu of South Africa 1885-1959* (Ohio University Press, 1997).

Hilton, J., 'The Classical Names Given to Slaves at the Western Cape in the Eighteenth Century', *Nomina Africana* 18 (1&2) (2004), 18-36.

Hilton, J., 'The Influence of Roman Law on the Practice of Slavery at the Cape of Good Hope', *Acta Classica* 50 (2007), 1-14.

Hilton, J., '*In Memoriam* Monica Anne Gosling (01.01.1944-14.08.2008)', *Akroterion* 53 (2008), 2-6.

Hilton, J. & Gosling, A. (eds), *Alma Parens Originalis? The Receptions of Classical*

Literature and Thought in Africa, Europe, the United States, and Cuba (Peter Lang, 2007).

Hingley, R., 'Francis John Haverfield (1860-1919): Oxford, Roman archaeology and Edwardian imperialism', in Stray C. *Oxford Classics* (Duckworth, 2007), 135-53.

Hose, M., '*Vaticinium Post Eventum* and the Position of the *Supplices* in the Danaid Trilogy', in D. Cairns & V. Liapis (eds), *Dionysalexandros: Essays on Aeschylus and his Fellow Tragedians in Honour of Alexander F. Garvie* (Classical Press of Wales, 2006), 91-8.

Hugo, A.M., '*In Piam Memoriam* Theodori J. Haarhoff 30.IV.1892-30.VIII. 1971', *Akroterion* 16 (4, 1971), 22-6 [followed by tributes by Baumbach and Smuts].

Isaac, B., *The Invention of Racism in Classical Antiquity* (Princeton University Press, 2004).

Jackson, J., '*In Memoriam*: Hansell Hewitt', *Akroterion* 34 (2, 1989), 160-1.

Klaaste, A., 'Great Africans of the Past', *The Argus*, October 10 (1995), 16.

Kollegas en Vriende, 'Professor C.P.T. Naudé, M.A. (Rand en Oxon), D. Litt et Phil. (Leiden) : 'N Waardering', *Acta Classica* 20 (1977), viii-xi.

Kriel, D.M., 'The Specification of Objectives', *Akroterion* 27 (3/4, 1982), 82-8.

Kriel, D.M., 'The Classics and the de Lange Report', *Akroterion* 28 (1/2, 1983), 3-10.

Kriel, D.M., '*In Memoriam* Henri Louis Gonin 3.12.1906-10.4.1997', *Acta Classica* 40 (1997), 1-3.

Kriel, D.M., '*In Memoriam* Huldeblyk aan Prof C.P.T Naudé (17.08.1912-10.08.2001), *Akroterion* 46 (2001), 3.

Lambert, M., 'The Classics: A Bridge between the Worlds', *Theoria* 73 (1989), 19-23.

Lambert, M., 'Nomkhubulwana: The Zulu Demeter', *Akroterion* 35 (2, 1990), 46-59.

Lambert, M., 'Ancient Greek and Zulu Sacrificial Ritual: A Comparative Analysis', *Numen* 40 (1993), 293-318.

Lambert, M., 'Ancient Greek and Traditional Zulu Medicine: A Question of Balance', *Acta Classica* 38 (1995), 71-87.

Lambert, M., 'Classical Athenian and Traditional African Ethics: The Hermeneutics of Shame and Guilt', *Southern African Journal for Folklore Studies* 11 (1, 2000), 41-55.

Lambert, M., 'Dr Mama Zainabu, Dr Swadik, and Ancient Greek Curses and Spells', in J. Hilton & A. Gosling (eds), *Alma Parens Originalis? The Receptions of Classical Literature and Thought in Africa, Europe, The United States, and Cuba* (Peter Lang, 2007), 117-33.

Lambert, M., 'Nomkhubulwane Reinventing a Zulu Goddess', in B. Carton, J. Laband & and J. Sithole (eds), *Zulu Identities: Being Zulu, Past and Present* (University of KwaZulu-Natal Press, 2008), 545-53.

Lambert, M. & Masoga, M.A., 'A Pan-African Response to the Classics', *Akroterion* 39 (2, 1994), 75-82.

Lloyd, M., 'The (F)utility of a Feminist Turn to Foucault', *Economy and Society* 22 (4, 1993), 437-60.

Lloyd-Jones, H., *Greek Epic, Lyric, and Tragedy* (Clarendon Press, 1990).

Lombard, D.B., '*In Memoriam* Charles August van Rooy', *Acta Classica* 41 (1998), 1-3.

Mackay, E.A., 'Classics in South Africa – A Way Forward', *Akroterion* 44 (1999), 79-90.

Mackinnon, J.K., 'The Reason for the Danaids' Flight', *Classical Quarterly* 28 (1978), 74-82.

Mandela, N., *Long Walk to Freedom: The Autobiography of Nelson Mandela* (Macdonald Purnell, 1994).

Mans, M., '*Laudatio*: D.M. Kriel', *Akroterion* 29 (1, 1984), 32-3.

Matier, K.O., '*In Memoriam* Sim Whiteley 4.12.1896-14.6.1986', *Acta Classica* 29 (1986), 1-2.

Bibliography

Matier, K.O., 'In Memoriam Sim Whiteley (4.12.1896-14.6.1986)', Akroterion 31 (2/3, 1986), 35-6.

Maylam, P. The Cult of Rhodes: Remembering an Imperialist in Africa (David Philip, 2005).

Meiring, P., 'Latyn het Henri Gonin jonk gehou', Akroterion 22 (1, 1977), 30-1.

Morris, A., 'Xénophobie à Johannesburg', in A. Bouillon (ed.), Immigration africaine en Afrique du Sud (Karthala, 1999).

Murgatroyd, P., 'Magnus Henderson: A Tribute', Akroterion 26 (3, 1981), 1-3.

Nienaber, G.S., Twee Taalstryders Pannevis en Preller (Nasou, 1967).

Nienaber, P.J., Notules Van Die Genootskap Van Regte Afrikaners 1875-1878 (Tafelberg, 1974).

Nienaber, P.J., Dr. Arnoldus Pannevis Vader van die Afrikaanse Taal (Nasionale Boekhandel, 1968).

Ntshangase, D.K., 'Between the Lion and the Devil: The Life and Works of B.W. Vilakazi, 1906-1947', Papers presented at seminars of the Institute for Advanced Social Research, University of the Witwatersrand, July-October 1995, 1-20.

NUX Student Newspaper, University of Natal, Pietermaritzburg (Students' Representative Council, UNP, 1972-1974, 1978, 1984).

O'Dowd, C., 'Obituary: Miss Elizabeth Cartwright', Akroterion 38 (2, 1993), 96.

Paap, A., 'In Memoriam Lydia Baumbach 1924-1991: A Personal Reflection', Acta Classica 34 (1991), 1-3.

Page, D. (ed.), Aeschylii Septem Quae Supersunt Tragoedias (Clarendon Press, 1972).

Parker, G., The Agony of Asar: A Thesis on Slavery by the Former Slave Jacobus Elisa Johannes Capitein 1717-1747 (Markus Wiener Publishers, 2001).

Pelling, C. (ed.), Greek Tragedy and the Historian (Clarendon Press, 1997).

Petrie, A., 'Professor T.J. Haarhoff – An Appreciation', Acta Classica 1 (1958), 9-13.

Phelan, S., 'Foucault and Feminism', American Journal of Political Science 34 (2, 1990), 421-40.

Podlecki, A.J., 'Reconstructing an Aeschylean Trilogy', Bulletin of the Institute of Classical Studies 22 (1975), 1-19.

Postma, J., ' 'n Lewensket van Prof. Dr. F. Postma', Akroterion 34 (3&4, 1989), 251-3.

Raven, D.S. The Role of Classical Studies in the 1970s (University of Natal Press, 1973).

Richards, W.J., 'In Memoriam Johannes Tobias Benade 20.04.1920-20.02.1988', Acta Classica 31 (1988), 1-3.

Richlin, A., 'Foucault's History of Sexuality: A Useful Theory for Women?' in D.H.J. Larmour, P.A. Miller & C. Platter (eds), Rethinking Sexuality: Foucault and Classical Antiquity (Princeton University Press, 1998), 138-70.

Rosen, K., 'C.P.T. Naudé als Gelehrter: Eine Würdigung', Acta Classica 20 (1977), xii-xv.

Rösler, W., 'Die Schluss der "Hiketiden" und die Danaiden-Trilogie des Aischylos'. Rheinisches Museum 136 (1993), 1-22.

Rotberg, R.I. (with the collaboration of Miles F. Shore), The Founder: Cecil Rhodes and the Pursuit of Power (Oxford University Press, 1988).

Saddington, D.B., 'Obituary – F.R.D. Goodyear', Akroterion 32 (3/4, 1987), 74.

Saddington, D.B., 'In Memoriam Charles P.T. Naudé', Acta Classica 44 (2001), 1-3.

Said, E.W., Orientalism (Penguin, 1995 repr.).

Sawicki, J., 'Foucault, Feminism, and Questions of Identity', in G. Gultong (ed.), The Cambridge Companion to Foucault (Cambridge University Press, 1994), 286-313.

Scourfield, J.H.D., 'The Classics After Apartheid', Classical Journal 88, 1992-1993, 43-54.

Scullion, S., 'Tragic Dates', Classical Quarterly 52 (1), 2002, 81-101.

Bibliography

Seaford, R., 'The Tragic Wedding', *Journal of the Hellenic Society* 107 (1987), 106-30.

Serfontein, J.H.P., *An Exposé of the Secret Afrikaner Broederbond* (Rex Collings Limited, 1979).

Shell, R.C-H., *Children of Bondage: A Social History of the Slave Society at the Cape of Good Hope, 1652-1838* (Witwatersrand University Press, 1994).

Shepherd, R.H.W., *Lovedale, South Africa: The Story of a Century 1841-1941* (The Lovedale Press, 1941).

Shillington, P., '*In Memoriam* Dorothy Farquharson Shillington', *Akroterion* (2, 1980), 30-1.

Sicherl, M. 'Die Tragik der Danaiden', *Museum Helveticum* 43 (1986), 81-110.

Smuts, F., 'Classical Scholarship and the Teaching of Classics at Cape Town and Stellenbosch', *Acta Classica* 3 (1960), 7-31.

Smuts, F., Review of W.J. Richards' *Gebed by Seneca. Acta Classica* 8 (1965), 124-9.

Smuts, F., 'J.P.J. van Rensburg', *Akroterion* 16 (4, 1971), 1-5.

Smuts, F., '*In Piam Memoriam* André Malan Hugo 13.6.29-24.1.75', *Akroterion* 20 (2/3, 1975), 1-5.

Smuts, F., '*In Memoriam* C.M.F. de Villiers 15.2.1952-4.10.1976', *Akroterion* 21 (3, 1976), 40-1.

Smuts, F., 'Johannes Petrus Janse van Rensburg', *Akroterion* 21 (4, 1976), 1-2.

Smuts, F., 'Die Klassieke in Suid-Afrika 1930-1976', *Akroterion* 21 (4, 1976), 11-21.

Smuts, F., '*In Memoriam* J.P.J. van Rensburg 23.8.1911-21.11.1980', *Akroterion* 25 (4, 1980), 1, 32.

Smuts, F., 'Henri Louis Gonin – 'n Waardering', *Acta Classica* 24 (1981), x-xiii.

Smuts, F., '*In Memoriam* Suretha Bruwer', *Akroterion* 29 (1, 1984), 1-2 [adapted from *Die Burger*, 27 October 1983; messages of condolence also published].

Smuts, F., '*In Memoriam* Susanna Margaretha Bruwer 10.10.1941-21.10.1983', *Acta Classica* 28 (1985), 1-4.

Sommerstein, A.H., 'The Theatre Audience, the *Demos*, and the *Suppliants* of Aeschylus', in C. Pelling (ed.), *Greek Tragedy and the Historian* (Clarendon, 1997).

Steinmeyer, E.G., *Plaintive Nightingale or Strident Swan? – The Reception of the Electra Myth from 1960-2005* (unpublished Ph.D. thesis, University of KwaZulu-Natal, 2007).

Steven, S.J.H., 'Professor Alexander Petrie M.A. (Aberdeen), B.A. (Cantab.), D.Litt. h.c. (Natal)', *Acta Classica* 2 (1959), 7-10.

Stray, C. (ed.), *Oxford Classics: Teaching and Learning, 1800-2000* (Duckworth, 2007).

Swanepoel, J., '*In Memoriam* A.G.P. van der Walt', *Acta Classica* 32 (1989), 1-2.

Swanepoel, J., '*In Memoriam*: A.G.P. van der Walt', *Akroterion* 34 (2, 1989), 162.

Tamarkin, M. *Cecil Rhodes and the Cape Afrikaners* (Frank Cass, 1996).

Thom. J., '*Curriculum Vitae* P.J. Conradie', *Akroterion* 41 (1/2, 1996), 3-4.

Thom, S. & Zietsman, J.C., '*In Memoriam* Albert (Bert) van Stekelenburg (31.03.1940-11.03.2003', *Akroterion* 47 (2002), 3.

Tutu, D., 'The South African Dream Revisited', *Weekend Witness*, September 30 2006, 10.

Van der Hoven, A., 'The Triumph of Method: J.M. Coetzee, the Humanities, South Africa', *Pretexts: Literary and Cultural Studies* 12 (1) (2003), 85-96.

Van Rensburg, J.P.J. 'Integer Vitae' (on Smuts' 60th birthday), *Akroterion* 21 (1, 1976), 1-2.

Van Rooij, C.A., 'In Memoriam: Professor S.J.H. Steven', *Acta Classica* 5 (1962), 1-2.

Van Stekelenburg, A.V., 'Latin in the Curriculum of Legal Studies in S.A. – Recent Developments and Projections', *Akroterion* 27 (3/4, 1982), 89, 161.

Van Stekelenburg, A.V., 'The Cape in Latin and Latin in the Cape in the 17th and 18th Centuries', *Akroterion* 48 (2003), 89-109.

Bibliography

Van Warmelo, P., 'Henri Gonin as Regsgeleerde', *Acta Classica* 24 (1981), xiv.

Van Zyl Smit, B., 'Medea and Apartheid', *Akroterion* 37 (2, 1992), 73-81.

Van Zyl Smit, B., '*Medea* in Afrikaans', in J. Hilton & A. Gosling (eds), *Alma Parens Originalis? The Receptions of Classical Literature and Thought in Africa, Europe, The United States, and Cuba* (Peter Lang, 2007), 73-91.

Van Zyl Smit, B., 'Multicultural Reception: Greek Drama in South Africa in the Late Twentieth and Early Twenty-First Centuries', in L. Hardwick & C. Stray (eds), *A Companion to Classical Receptions* (Blackwell Publishing, 2008), 373-85.

Vasunia, P., *The Gift of the Nile: Hellenizing Egypt from Aeschylus to Alexander* (University of California Press, 2001).

Vasunia, P., 'Greater Rome and Greater Britain', in B. Goff (ed.), *Classics and Colonialism* (Duckworth, 2005), 38-64.

Vidal-Naquet, P., 'The Place and Status of Foreigners in Athenian Tragedy', in C. Pelling (ed.), *Greek Tragedy and the Historian* (Clarendon Press, 1997), 109-19.

Vigouroux, C.B., ' "J'ai trop de langues dans ma tête". Enquête sur les pratiques et les representations linguistiques des migrants africains francophones de la ville du Cap', in A. Bouillon (ed.), *Immigration africaine en Afrique du Sud* (Karthala, 1999).

Wakerley, M., 'Latin at the University of Transkei', *Akroterion* 27 (3/4, 1982), 97-103.

Wakerley, M., 'Law Students Like Latin – The Unitra Latin Course', *Akroterion* 30 (4, 1985), 100-3.

Wardle, D., 'The Rhodes Collection A National Asset', *Akroterion* 38 (1993), 86-91.

Wardle, D., 'John Edward Atkinson: An Appreciation', *Acta Classica* 48 (2005), vii-xi.

Weedon, C., *Feminist Practice and Poststructuralist Theory* (Blackwell, 2004, repr.).

Weideman, B.P., *Die posisie van Latyn as vak aan sekondêre skole in die RSA* (Raad vir Geesteswetenskaplike Navorsing, 1984).

Whitaker, R., *Homer and Orality and Literacy in Ancient Greece* (University of Cape Town, 1990).

Whitaker, R., 'The Classics in South African Society – Past, Present and Future', *Acta Classica* 40 (1997), 5-14.

Whitaker, R., '*In Memoriam* Margaret (Maggie) Rosabel Mezzabotta 17.07.1946-20.02.2000', *Acta Classica* 43 (2000), 1-3.

Whitaker, R., 'Tribute to Margaret Rosabel Mezzabotta (17.07.1946-20.02.2000)', *Akroterion* 45 (2000), 3 [followed by a poem in Afrikaans by Joan Hambidge, translated into English by the author].

White, K.D. (ed.), Hemmy, *De Promontorio Bonae Spei* (South African Public Library, 1959).

Williams, B., *Cecil Rhodes* (Constable and Company, 1938).

Win, E., 'An Alien in Jozi', *Mail & Guardian* 20 (40), 2004, 18.

Winnington-Ingram, R.P., *Studies in Aeschylus* (Cambridge University Press, 1983).

Wiseman, T.P., *Talking to Virgil* (University of Exeter Press, 1992).

Woodward, K., *Understanding Identity* (Arnold, 2002).

Zeitlin, F.I., *Playing the Other: Gender and Society in Classical Greek Literature* (University of Chicago Press, 1996).

Zelenak, M.X., *Gender and Politics in Greek Tragedy* (Peter Lang, 1998).

Index

53333485R00091

Made in the USA
Middletown, DE
27 November 2017